Owning Intelligence

How AI is Reshaping Intellectual Property, Risk, and Governance

Jennifer C. Wolfe
Nancy E. Cronin

Apress®

Owning Intelligence: How AI is Reshaping Intellectual Property, Risk, and Governance

Jennifer C. Wolfe
Hilton Head Island, SC, USA

Nancy E. Cronin
Jericho, VT, USA

ISBN-13 (pbk): 979-8-8688-2387-9
ISBN-13 (electronic): 979-8-8688-2388-6
https://doi.org/10.1007/979-8-8688-2388-6

Managing Director, Apress Media LLC: Welmoed Spahr
Acquisitions Editor: Susan McDermott
Project Manager: Jessica Vakili

Distributed to the book trade worldwide by Springer Science+Business Media New York, 1 New York Plaza, New York, NY 10004. Phone 1-800-SPRINGER, fax (201) 348-4505, e-mail orders-ny@springer-sbm.com, or visit www.springeronline.com. Apress Media, LLC is a Delaware LLC and the sole member (owner) is Springer Science + Business Media Finance Inc (SSBM Finance Inc). SSBM Finance Inc is a **Delaware** corporation.

For information on translations, please e-mail booktranslations@springernature.com; for reprint, paperback, or audio rights, please e-mail bookpermissions@springernature.com.

Apress titles may be purchased in bulk for academic, corporate, or promotional use. eBook versions and licenses are also available for most titles. For more information, reference our Print and eBook Bulk Sales web page at http://www.apress.com/bulk-sales.

If disposing of this product, please recycle the paper

Table of Contents

About the Authors

Jennifer C. Wolfe, Esq., APR, SSBB, is an internationally recognized expert on intellectual property (IP) strategy, corporate governance, and emerging technologies. She is the founder and executive director of the Governing Intelligence Research Group. She was a founder and managing partner of one of the largest woman-owned boutique IP law firms in the United States and later launched Dot Brand 360, a digital strategy consultancy which she successfully exited after a decade of advising global brands.

Jen has served as the chair of the Independent Review of ICANN's (Internet Corporation for Assigned Names and Numbers) Generic Names Supporting Organization (GNSO), advising on international internet governance policy, and has been a faculty member and leadership fellow for the National Association of Corporate Directors (NACD) on digital transformation and risk.

A prolific author of six IP and governance books, Forbes Business Council contributor, and keynote speaker, Jen brings thought leadership spanning Fortune 100 boardrooms, international policy forums, and fast-growing startups. Her focus now lies in helping boards, general counsel, and executives navigate the evolving frontier of AI, organizational behavior, and intellectual asset management (IAM).

Nancy E. Cronin, PE, is a strategy expert, engineer, and innovation consultant who advises leading companies across a diverse set of industries. With deep expertise in intellectual asset management, IP strategy, invention portfolio development, and patent analytics, Nancy brings a unique perspective at the intersection of technical invention and legal protection.

Her work spans the full lifecycle of innovation from ideation and analytics to invention harvesting, documentation and strategic advisement, and, most recently, AI integration into IP workflows. She has guided Fortune 500 companies in building defendable IP portfolios and identifying whitespace and has been recognized repeatedly for 10 years among the *IAM Strategy 300: The World's Leading IP Strategists.*

Nancy's technical education from Caltech and Harvard, her background in engineering and IP strategy, and her 25-year career as a recognized IP professional allow her to bridge the divide between engineering teams and legal departments, making her a sought-after advisor and facilitator for interdisciplinary innovation strategy challenges.

Prologue

This book began nearly a year ago, after a simple lunch that turned into a wide-ranging conversation about careers, families, and what comes next in our lives. Both of us have had a decades-long career in intellectual property (IP) so, inevitably, the discussion drifted toward artificial intelligence (AI) and the possibility of collaborating to write a book. From the start, we knew the task would be daunting. To write about a field moving at breakneck speed means accepting that much of what we describe will evolve, even become obsolete before these pages ever reach a reader. Still, our goal was not to capture the fleeting headlines of the moment, but to consider the deeper currents: the paradigm shifts of the past, the principles of governance, and the enduring question of ownership.

The pace of technological development ensures that by the time this goes to press, some details will already feel outdated. But the structural questions, who owns the intelligence that powers our future, how it is governed, and how unintended consequences are contained, will remain central. If history has taught us anything, it is that those who control the core platforms of technology also control extraordinary influence. We've seen this already in the rise of Google, Apple, Microsoft, Meta, Amazon, and others: companies that hold vast troves of data, dictate algorithms that make or break small businesses, and shape not just consumer behavior, but political and cultural life.

Now, imagine what happens when the next generation of AI embeds itself everywhere: our cars, homes, workplaces, supply chains, health systems, and even our very biology. It may monitor our sleep patterns, anticipate what we eat, analyze our genetic code, and, in Orwellian fashion, infer what we think. In the coming decades, the intelligence woven into devices, robots, and networks will not merely serve us; it will shape the very contours of human experience. How we govern this transition will determine whether it elevates humanity or diminishes it.

At the heart of this challenge is intellectual property. Who owns what AI creates? Who owns the data and content fed into these systems, and what information is acceptable to use? Who is accountable when things go wrong? These questions are not merely academic but needed to implement the essential policies needed. Every company will deploy AI. Some will build it, others will buy or license it, but all will depend on it in some way. Without clear structures for ownership, governance, and risk management, organizations risk chaos and society risks harm.

This is not a problem for coders alone. Today, brilliant young developers are creating technologies that will define the century, but they cannot be expected to foresee every unintended consequence. There are larger issues of ethics, legality, and brand. That responsibility falls to senior leaders, policymakers, and lawyers and to those with the experience to recognize the stakes. Just as the framers of the US Constitution laid down a foundation for more than two centuries of self-governance, the builders and implementers of AI today have a duty to establish principles of ownership, governance, and accountability that can guide generations to come.

The opportunity and the responsibility lie before us. The decisions made in the next decade will shape not just markets, but humanity itself.

CHAPTER 1

Why We Wrote This Book and What You'll Gain from It

Artificial intelligence is rapidly transforming how we work, create, and compete, but the rules governing how we protect what is created and how it is created are not evolving nearly as fast. As consultants, legal strategists, engineers, and governance experts, we've witnessed firsthand how disruptive AI is to the intellectual property (IP) landscape. Companies are building faster, with smarter tools, but often without clear guidance on how to secure what they create or what risks they may unknowingly inherit.

We wrote this book because we saw a gap. A critical one.

There are countless books on artificial intelligence. Some focus on ethics. Others on the future of work. Still others dive deep into the technical foundations of machine learning or the public policy debates surrounding it. But what's been missing is a practical, implementation-focused guide for business leaders, in-house legal teams, engineers, and directors on how to navigate the intersection of IP, innovation, and governance in the AI era.

J. C. Wolfe and N. E. Cronin, *Owning Intelligence*,
https://doi.org/10.1007/979-8-8688-2388-6_1

AI is now both a creator and a risk: Every time your team uses an AI tool, you may be generating intellectual property or exposing it. You might be using someone else's protected content in a training dataset or creating original outputs that aren't protected because your policies or contracts don't account for AI. The liabilities are real and the opportunities are enormous. And very few organizations are prepared for either.

Governance is critical to managing AI now and in the future: Fear about an AI apocalypse is no longer just science fiction, but a scenario some have carefully mapped out as AI breaks free of laws and policy. Strong oversight, governance and guardrails go hand in hand with the intellectual assets upon which AI is built and the outputs it creates. Every organization, large and small, will need governance, process, and policy around its use and deployment of AI. Yet, according to studies by PwC and EY, only 11% of executives believe they are implementing responsible practices despite 95% saying they are investing in it. Microsoft's Work Trend Index estimates that 78% of employees bring their own AI tools into the workplace. Without process and accountability, it is the Wild West of AI usage. While these numbers will change, executives are looking for guidance beyond just a well-written policy. A few of the types of AI governance that will be needed include:

- Board and Executive Oversight
- Technical Guardrails in AI Development
- Employee Use and Acceptable AI Policy
- Intellectual Property and Data Governance
- Regulatory and Ethical Compliance
- Vendor and Third-Party AI Oversight
- Incident and Crisis Management

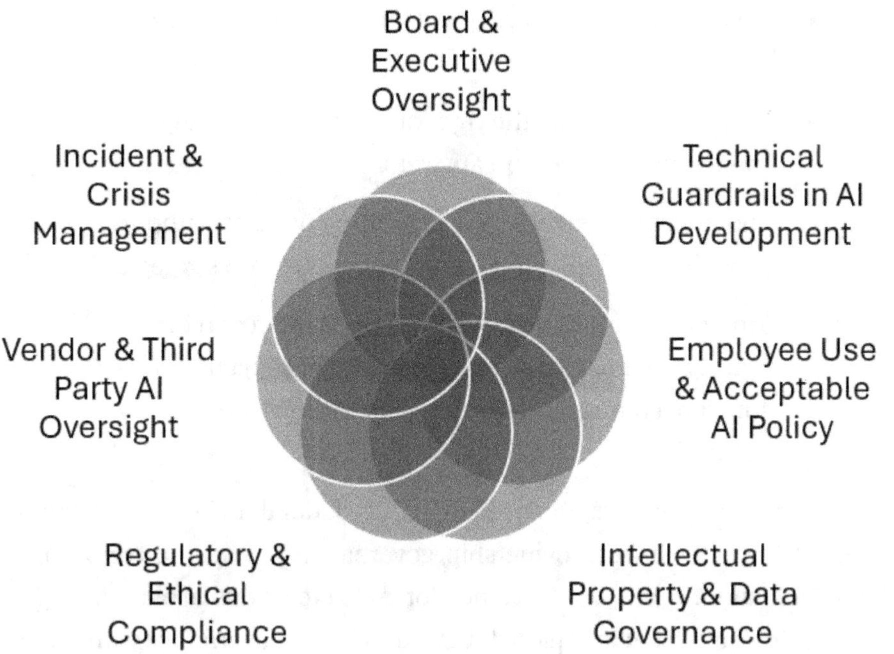

We're entering the AI era as a new industrial revolution. Where the industrial revolution made IP law necessary, the AI revolution will make IP process essential. Every company will need to strategically protect what you create while ensuring you don't infringe on others and responsibly implement AI. The future will largely rest on the power of AI combined with human connection and engagement. Together they form the next wave of intellectual assets that will power society.

Why We Wrote This Together

Our collaboration began from a shared concern that businesses, even sophisticated ones, were underprepared to manage the new reality of AI-generated and AI-assisted work. As professionals who've built careers in law, innovation consulting, engineering, and IP strategy, we recognized that:

- Legal frameworks were being outpaced by technical advances.
- Boards were asking the right questions, but getting vague or sometimes no answers.
- Too many organizations were writing policies without processes or deploying AI without ownership strategies.
- Worst of all, many companies simply are frozen in place, either not knowing what to do or plugging in software solutions and workflows without process or cultural buy-in.

We knew the conversation needed to be broader than just compliance or ethics. It needed to include ownership, governance, process, and real-world implementation. That's why we joined forces to create this book; bringing together Jen's experience in global IP law and board governance with Nancy's expertise in engineering, patent strategy, and AI technical systems.

How We Researched This Book: A Human-AI Collaboration

We approached this book like we recommend organizations approach AI: thoughtfully, strategically, and with clarity around human vs. AI roles.

- **Traditional research**: We reviewed court decisions, legislation, global regulatory frameworks (such as the EU AI Act and US Federal regulatory guidance), academic journals, and case law related to copyright, trade secret, and patent law. Our references include publicly available information about real-world licensing deals, infringement claims, and governance frameworks.

- **AI-assisted research**: We used AI tools to aggregate news sources, identify patent trends, organize data, and draft early summaries or outlines for certain sections. Generative tools helped us identify recurring themes and locate edge cases that might otherwise have been buried in search results. This was followed by fact-checking to avoid AI "hallucinations."
- **Interviews**: We interviewed people in the trenches of using AI across organizations to understand their viewpoints and concerns and learn what's anecdotally happening out there every day.
- **Human oversight and original thinking**: Every chapter, structure, and argument was designed, curated, and critically refined by us. AI did not write this book. It helped us explore possibilities faster. It helped us edit. It helped us create tables and put together alphabetized lists of the research we conducted. But it was human expertise, legal reasoning, professional judgment, and industry insight that drove what to include, how to explain it, and what we believe matters most to you as a reader.

This dual approach mirrors what we recommend for any organization using AI: leverage automation to support creativity and insight, but always with human guidance, oversight, and accountability.

What This Book Covers

In the chapters that follow, we'll take you through

- **How IP law intersects with AI technology** and why foundational models and generative tools have upended traditional approaches to ownership and authorship

- **Real case studies** in copyright, patent law, and trade secret disputes involving AI
- **Practical strategies** for detecting infringement in AI-generated content using emerging software tools
- **Guidance on what can be patented** and what is better protected as a trade secret in AI workflows
- **Model policies and governance frameworks** that boards and executives can implement now
- **Questions for directors** and legal teams to assess risk and prepare for regulatory scrutiny
- **Checklists and templates** for managing employee, third-party, and vendor use of AI tools
- And most importantly, a playbook for how to **build AI-informed governance and IP strategies** that protect your innovations rather than expose them

What You'll Gain from This Book

Our goal is to help you answer the questions you may already be asking and some you haven't thought of yet:

- *Who owns what we're creating with AI tools?*
- *Is our training data infringing someone else's rights?*
- *What role should our board play in AI risk oversight?*
- *Do our vendor contracts protect us if they use AI improperly?*
- *Are we losing trade secrets every time an employee uses an AI tool?*
- *What systems can we build now to avoid lawsuits later?*

- *What new organizational systems and processes do we need?*
- *Where should this reside and how do we manage this complex new environment?*

This book will not give you generic legal boilerplate or abstract philosophy. It will give you frameworks, real examples, and actionable strategies to help you

- Protect what your company builds
- Avoid accidental infringement
- Align your IP strategy with AI development
- Train your teams to use AI responsibly
- Help your board and executives meet their duty of care

If you're in legal, governance, innovation, compliance, or product development, this book is for you. If you're asking "what should we be doing about AI and IP?", this book is for you. If you're already working with AI tools and wondering if your contracts, policies, and strategies are future-proof, this book is for you.

In Closing: A Turning Point for Innovation

We believe we are standing at a turning point. Despite current challenges in securing the hard resources such as chips and land, energy and water for data centers and essential for growth, use of AI will not slow down. If anything, it will accelerate. Some will leverage it to the fullest potential and expand and scale their businesses and careers as a result. Others may find themselves displaced or exposed as ill-prepared. The organizations that win in this era will not be the ones that use AI the most but the ones that use it wisely, strategically, and with an ownership mindset.

We hope this book helps you become one of them.

Let's begin.

CHAPTER 2

Understanding Artificial Intelligence in the Context of IP

A (Very) Brief History of AI and How It Has Evolved

What is Artificial Intelligence (AI)? Believe it or not, AI is not a new concept.

The term dates back to the mid-1950s when Marvin Minsky of Harvard University and John McCarthy of Dartmouth College created a proposal, along with Nathaniel Rochester from IBM and Claude Shannon from Bell Telephone Laboratories, titled "A Proposal for the Dartmouth Summer Research Project on Artificial Intelligence." In the summer of 1956, nearly 50 people participated in the workshop on the topic. It is generally considered to be the "birth" of the term "artificial intelligence" in the United States.

Other researchers outside of the United States further provided a foundation for the emergence of AI. Notably the efforts of individuals including Alan Turing, W. Grey Walter, Konrad Zuse, and Anatoly Kitov predate Minsky and McCarthy and likely informed or influenced the

J. C. Wolfe and N. E. Cronin, *Owning Intelligence*,
https://doi.org/10.1007/979-8-8688-2388-6_2

thinking of Minsky and McCarthy. While it is beyond the scope of this book to provide a detailed history of AI development and its varied contributors, suffice to say that AI has evolved over decades of global advancements in computer science, programming, and the underlying hardware that delivers the current results of AI tools.

AI may not be new; however, it has rapidly become omnipresent in news, articles, and social media.

Technical Evolution of Intellectual Property Protection

Meanwhile, IP has experienced its own evolution over the past several decades. Technology has played a significant role in how IP processing has advanced from physical and paper methods to digital. Of course, inventions also have been highly influenced by technological advancements. Inventions that cover all varieties of software and hardware solutions have become part of the more than 12 million patents granted by the United States Patent and Trademark Office (USPTO).

From 2000 to the present, a series of key events have occurred in the IP protection process that have heavily impacted the way technology companies behave with respect to IP. This is relevant to the AI conversation, because today's inventions, whether created to protect an AI-related concept or created using AI tool support, will become the next IP milestone in the chronology of IP protection history.

We expect the volume and character of protected inventions to change dramatically based on rapid development of content, using AI to accelerate a company's ability to conceptualize, document, refine and file a patent application.

See below a timeline of events that are particularly relevant to tech companies and also to patent applicants who use various forms of technology support in their inventions. The timeline illustrates how the IP protection process has evolved from an era focused on patent volume, software patent expansion, and defensive filing into a more complex global strategy shaped by litigation, regulation, market competition, and emerging technologies. Key legal decisions such as eBay v. MercExchange, the America Invents Act, and Alice v. CLS Bank changed how companies file, challenge, enforce, and value patents, while the smartphone patent wars demonstrated how IP could become a core competitive asset. More recent developments, including China's stronger IP enforcement, pandemic-era IP sharing, Europe's Unified Patent Court, and debates over AI-generated inventions. These activities and events show that modern IP strategy continues to require speed, technical precision, international coordination, and flexibility in choosing between patents, trade secrets, licensing, and open innovation - and utilize all available technological advances.

Timeline of Technologies That Have Shaped the IP Protection Process

1 Early–2000s Software Patent Expansion & Rising Reexamination Activity

- USPTO increased reexaminations and more software patents were filed
- Tech companies filed aggressively to protect territory and deter copycats.
- IBM led with 3,000+ patent filings in 2001.

2 2006 – eBay Inc. v. MercExchange Supreme Court Decision

- Patent holders could no longer automatically get injunctions.
- Reduced leverage of non-practicing entities ("patent trolls").
- Operating companies shifted toward licensing strategies.
- Microsoft expanded cross-licensing and defensive aggregation through AST.

3 2011 – America Invents Act (AIA)

- Signed in September 2011; fully implemented in 2013.
- Shifted U.S. patent law from "first to invent" to "first to file" and introduced IPR.
- Speed to file and post-grant challenges became crucial.
- Patents became front-line competitive tools.

4 2012–2014 – Smartphone Patent Wars

- High-profile battles, especially Apple v. Samsung, over smartphone features and design.
- Patents became front-line competitive tools.
- Companies built portfolios for litigation leverage and licensing.
- Google bought Motorola Mobility in 2012 for $12.5B and 17,000+ patents.

5 2014 – Alice Corp. v. CLS Bank Supreme Court Decision

- Limited patentability of abstract ideas, especially in software and fintech.
- Many software patents became weaker or harder to enforce.
- Companies shifted toward narrower, more technical claims.

6 2018 – China IP Enforcement Surge

- China created specialized IP courts and strengthened patent protection.
- Filing in China became more strategic for global companies.
- Foreign filings and domestic enforcement increased.
- Qualcomm won injunctions against Apple in China in 2018.

7 2020 – COVID-19 and the IP Sharing Wave

- Pandemic urgency encouraged IP sharing for medical technologies.
- Fueled debate over IP flexibility and responsible innovation.
- Companies balanced patent protection with open innovation.
- IBM, Amazon, and Microsoft joined the Open COVID Pledge.

8 2023 – Unitary Patent & Unified Patent Court in Europe

- Europe introduced the Unitary Patent and UPC.
- Enforcement across EU member states became simpler.
- Centralized litigation risk also increased.
- Siemens and other multinationals prepared coordinated strategies.

9 2023–Present – AI-Generated Inventions and IP Debates

- Debate continues over whether AI systems can be inventors, including DABUS cases.
- Protectability of AI-generated ideas remains uncertain.
- Companies are revising inventor policies and exploring trade secrets or copyrights.

Core AI Technologies That Have IP Impacts

It is helpful to know what underlying technologies are being used within the most common AI tools available today. Here are brief definitions of generative AI (GenAI) and large language models (LLMs).

Generative AI

Generative AI (GenAI) is a category of AI that creates new content, such as text, music, designs, or computer code, that didn't exist before, based on patterns it learned from training data. A variety of learning models are used for GenAI, and they are not all text based.

While an in-depth summary is beyond the scope of this book, you should minimally know that a variety of models exist to provide the training "engine" for generative AI, and they are selected based on the use and purpose of the tool. Some are used for language, as for large language models, but others are used for music, speech, images, etc.

One point to be aware of regarding generative AI is that its results *may incorporate or resemble the data with which it was trained.* That is because it learns from examples, that is, the training data. This can pose IP ownership or infringement concerns, particularly if the training data includes proprietary content. A further concern is how to maintain secrecy of data that you don't want to become part of a training corpus of information for generative AI tools. We will cover this in more detail in later chapters.

Large Language Models (LLMs)

Large language models (LLMs) are advanced computer systems trained to understand and generate human-like text. They are designed to read, comprehend, and respond to written language. LLMs can process tremendous amounts of data, well beyond what a human can do quickly, to predict and produce responses in the form of human-like text.

LLMs are trained using deep learning, a form of machine learning that mimics the human brain's structure with artificial "neurons." They are fed huge datasets made up of content, such as books, articles, and websites, and "learn" (associate) patterns in how words are used and combined. During training, the LLM guesses the next word in a sentence, repeatedly, until the model gets very good at predicting context and meaning. Once trained, an LLM can write emails, summarize reports, or explain complex ideas in plain language.

Something you may not know is that LLMs don't "understand" language like a human being. They instead predict patterns. It may seem like an LLM is thinking, but it is in fact predicting the next word based on everything that came before it by recognizing word patterns and associations. This necessitates strict fact-checking and human oversight. You may have heard of "AI hallucinations." You'll always get an answer back from an LLM, but it may not be based on facts!

Image and Media Generation Tools

Images and videos can now be created quickly and directly using AI tools, using inputs such as text prompts or visual references. Instead of requiring specialized design skills or traditional production methods, these tools allow a user to describe what they want to see or provide a sample image with desired changes, and the AI tool will generate the corresponding media. This shift is making creative content production faster, more accessible, and increasingly cost efficient.

A key element in how these tools work lies in the connection between language models and generative image models. Language models interpret the user's instructions, capturing nuance, context, and intent, while generative models translate that understanding into visual outputs. The language model acts as an "interpreter," ensuring the system understands the request, and the image model acts as the "artist," producing the result.

Some examples of tools that illustrate this new capability include Midjourney, DALL-E, Stable Diffusion (an open-source alternative), and Google's Imagen. These platforms are rapidly changing how companies can approach marketing, product design, training, and communications.

These tools typically rely on models like **diffusion models** (e.g., Stable Diffusion or DALL-E), which begin with random noise and slowly "improve" the image to match the prompt. They are trained on massive datasets containing images and their captions, learning how to connect words and visual features. Over time, the model learns to "imagine" (rather, they are improving results drawn on training data) and create realistic or stylized visuals that reflect a concept or brand vision.

These tools can be used to accelerate visual concept development for advertising, product packaging, or virtual prototypes. A tech startup, for example, might use image or video generation tools to visualize a product that hasn't been built yet. However, it should be noted that copyright protection and ownership of AI-generated images is tricky and has specific requirements to allow for IP protection. The Supreme Court determined in 2026 that AI cannot be an author under US copyright law, and works created autonomously by AI *without* meaningful human creative input cannot be copyrighted.

An interesting insight is that an image generation tool doesn't understand or "see" images. The tools start with a random static image and iterate it to adjust the pixels through hundreds of steps to eventually match what the prompt (input text) describes. The process is very statistical (math based) and can lead to strange and unexpected results, even with small changes in the text prompt.

AI Agents and Agentic AI

The most recent developments in AI tools are how they are rapidly being combined, and automated, to take action with very little or no oversight from a human. This has tremendous implications on governance, oversight, and ethics and leads to many questions about IP ownership, authorship, and management.

To differentiate between the two, AI agents are autonomous software systems that can perform tasks on behalf of humans. An AI agent doesn't just follow fixed rules, but can use the sources researched and proceed to interpret context, make decisions, and adapt as they work.

For example, an AI agent designed for customer service operations might receive and manage incoming customer messages, classify them by urgency, draft and send responses, and escalate only the more complex cases to human staff.

Agentic AI takes an AI agent a step further. In this case, the system doesn't just execute discrete tasks but in essence acts independently toward a goal. Agentic AI often draws on multiple AI agents and can connect multiple steps together, dynamically make decisions, and coordinate with other agents or systems. It essentially "decides what to do next."

An agentic AI example in supply chain management might run logistics for the company, including monitoring and prediction of material shortages, creating purchase orders, and ordering what is needed, and even monitoring and rerouting shipments in real time.

Why does this matter? Because AI agents are moving from decision support to decision execution. This shift brings both opportunity and risk when considering IP, as the AI agents and agentic AI operate across multiple systems, APIs, and datasets, which may contain licensed, confidential, or copyrighted material. This could prove to be even more difficult to manage than directing employee behavior, as the traceability of the data sources for an AI agent or agentic AI may not be transparent.

The Importance of Proprietary Data

As mentioned above, the use of AI tools can lead to inadvertent (or intentional) misuse of data ownership.

While the opportunities for AI use are compelling, these opportunities also introduce critical business risks. IP concerns can arise because the models are trained on datasets that may include copyrighted or trademarked materials, raising uncertainty over originality and ownership of generated outputs. Cases such as The New York Times v. OpenAI and Microsoft and Getty Images v. Stability AI and are becoming more frequent and are likely the tip of the iceberg for data ownership tussles.

Data ownership presents another set of challenges: if employees input proprietary documents, customer information, or product concepts into generative AI tools, it is not always clear how that data will be stored, used, or repurposed and whether it could inadvertently contribute to further training of the model. Unless companies have established boundaries around both the tools and the employee behavior using them, there is risk that may lead to negative consequences for brand reputation, competitive positioning, and compliance with data protection regulations. Many AI tool platforms allow for limiting use as training data, but unless a company has that type of subscription, sensitive data could be flowing back to the AI platform for training and further use.

For these reasons, companies must recognize that the adoption of generative AI and media creation tools is a matter not only of how useful or capable they can be but also of governance.

To safeguard against IP mishaps and data misuse, organizations need clear internal guidance on how these tools should and should not be used. Establishing and enforcing such guidance is essential to ensure that innovation is pursued responsibly, without exposing the business to avoidable legal, regulatory, or reputational harm. This leads us to the next chapter, "Ownership and Authorship of AI."

Key Takeaways

- AI is not a new concept. Its roots trace back to the 1950s with foundational work by researchers like John McCarthy and Alan Turing, and its current form reflects decades of global technical evolution.
- Intellectual property law has evolved in parallel with technology. Key events from software patent expansion in the early 2000s to the America Invents Act and the rise of global patent systems have shaped how tech companies create, protect, and defend innovation.
- AI now accelerates the volume and speed of invention. Companies can conceptualize, refine, and file patent applications faster using AI-supported workflows, which will reshape what types of inventions enter the IP system.
- Major patent law milestones (e.g., Alice Corp. v. CLS Bank, AIA reforms, global IP courts) influence whether AI-driven ideas qualify for protection and how companies structure their portfolios and filing strategies.
- Core AI technologies, generative AI, large language models, diffusion models, and AI agents fundamentally change how content and solutions are produced, raising new IP risks and opportunities.
- Generative models can unintentionally reproduce features from training data, introducing infringement and confidentiality risks if proprietary or copyrighted content was used.

- Visual and media generation tools (Midjourney, DALL-E, Stable Diffusion) expand creative capabilities but require new guardrails to manage ownership and originality.
- AI agents and agentic systems increase autonomy and opacity, making governance and tracking of data sources, authorship, and liability significantly more complex.
- Proprietary data is now a critical IP asset and a liability. Without guidance, employees may unknowingly expose trade secrets or copyrighted content through AI tools.
- The intersection of AI and IP is now about governance as much as innovation. Responsible use requires internal policy, oversight of data inputs, and risk controls to protect brand, ownership rights, and regulatory compliance.

CHAPTER 3

Ownership and Authorship of AI

As AI becomes an inseparable part of both the creation and commercialization of products and services, organizations face new IP complexities. Who owns an AI-generated work? How should a company protect the proprietary data used to train or prompt an AI? And what happens when AI-driven processes (knowingly or unknowingly) infringe on existing IP?

This chapter explores five aspects of these questions:

(1) The distinction between AI-generated and AI-assisted works and the IP implications of each

(2) The strategic treatment of data as a proprietary asset

(3) The evolving landscape of infringement detection and liability in AI-generated outputs

(4) The role of patents in protecting AI-enabled innovation

(5) A short preview of the critical policies and processes companies must adopt to maintain control, reduce risk, and protect value

J. C. Wolfe and N. E. Cronin, *Owning Intelligence*,
https://doi.org/10.1007/979-8-8688-2388-6_3

These factors will drive new and evolving organizational structure, policy, process, and procedure. Proactive governance will quickly become a must-have in a world where AI is intermingled with human-created and managed content. For executive leaders now is the time to begin developing a plan that is ready to implement.

As a final thought, consider the implications of human involvement needed to create assets that can be scaled and protected and whether or not changing laws will change this requirement. Will your organization play a pivotal role in that policy development?

AI-Generated Works, AI-Assisted Works, and the Underlying Data As IP

Policies for Use by Employees

Without guidelines, there is no telling how your employees will use AI in their daily job responsibilities. So, it is advisable for a company to establish policies in order to both reap the benefits of AI use and protect against costly blunders. The lack of setting an AI policy risks potential IP losses that may not be recoverable and the loss of brand value via AI-generated errors.

Most tech-savvy employees are already using various forms of AI (such as ChatGPT or Claude). However, there also remain many employees who are confused or afraid of its use. Here are some suggestions for management policies that are designed to help standardize the education level of your team and provide practical guidance on the uses of AI:

1. Train your team on the basics of AI so that they recognize instances of when it should or should not be used. Education will go a long way to engender not just compliance but enthusiasm for smart AI use that protects the company.

- **Example**: Without fact-checking, AI tools are notorious for providing incorrect financial information. The use of AI for citing figures to include in annual reports or other business reporting documents should be avoided or minimally must be double-checked to avoid embarrassing or even material blunders.

2. Create clear guidelines on which AI tools are approved for use and under what circumstances. This may include specific tools that the company subscribes to, what specific areas of the company will be utilizing AI tools, and, more importantly, where they should *not* be used. Educate employees on risks of using free or unvetted AI platforms that may not guarantee IP ownership.

    - **Example**: "Our company supports the use of AI for marketing research, but only under the supervision of the marketing director and needs to be conducted using the corporate and data-protected subscription to Open AI."

Note In the absence of specific company guidance, your employees are likely using AI without corporate knowledge or consent. We have heard anecdotally that employees will use a personal AI platform of preference when not provided access to AI or feel overly constrained by the tools made available to them.

---

3. For teams that use AI to support creation of potentially patentable concepts, implement capture processes for AI-assisted outputs that are integrated into concept development, R&D, and product development.

    - **Example**: A research team uses AI tools to search for and expand technical operability for inventions. A standard operating procedure is implemented to document the prompts used, the output report, and the sources cited that are incorporated into R&D efforts.

Policies Around Third-Party-Provided Support

Modern companies often rely on support beyond their internal team to accomplish tasks, especially if they lie outside of the core competencies of the team, require speed, or are beyond the ability for the internal team to handle. Third-party contracts are commonplace. However, the use of AI by those third parties may not be immediately evident to you. Your company needs to review standard third-party contracts, update them with AI related IP controls, and provide oversight to ensure your company policies are followed.

Examples of this might include:

- Require vendor agreements to explicitly transfer ownership of AI-generated outputs to the client.
- Mandate IP indemnification clauses to mitigate the risk of unintentional infringement.
    - For example, what if the third party either intentionally or unintentionally use proprietary information through an AI tool to provide a work product?

    - There are examples such as the ongoing Photobucket litigation, which alleges the company was collecting and using biometric identifiers without informed, written consent and may be "selling or profiting from" biometric data.

- Validate the origin of any training data used by third-party AI providers to avoid downstream liability.
    - If the third party is using your data for development of a work product, ensure that this information is not used for their other clients.

AI As Work for Hire

The idea of "work for hire" is well known; however, it may be less known how to handle AI-developed outputs and may not be covered in your current contracts. Third-party contracts should dictate ownership of AI-developed outputs. Contracts need to clearly define ownership of outputs, when AI tools are developed by or deployed by external vendors. This may be an IP negotiation point with third parties (i.e., whether you or they own AI outputs in a given situation). Inside your company, clear delineation of AI-generated output can avoid future confusion and disputes.

Ensure that "employee-generated AI outputs" are covered under existing work-for-hire or IP assignment agreements with your employees. In some cases, your company may need to classify whether AI systems trained internally fall under company-owned IP or require a new special classification, particularly if your system is to be shared or used by third parties.

While it may often seem that AI produces information without effort, the results can carry tremendous value – **which should be regarded as your IP.**

Garbage In, Garbage Out: The nuances of Human-Generated Prompts and Revisions

It is well known that any computing system that relies on inputs to generate outputs requires good information on the front end to lead to accurate and useful information on the back end. Large language models are no different. Some of your employees are likely honing skills at interacting with AI platforms such as ChatGPT and are becoming increasingly skilled at generating prompts within your company's areas of expertise.

The newly emerging concept of "prompt development" is not only a necessity for getting good results from generative AI platforms; it further provides a company a valuable opportunity to manage and protect the unique knowledge and learnings embodied in this activity.

Here are a few recommendations for how to protect the information being developed in your organization and establish new policies and procedures to normalize the use of AI in a controlled fashion:

1. **Treat high-value prompts and refined workflows as proprietary assets subject to protection.**

   High-value prompts (prompts that are developed, and likely iterated, refined, tested, and improved by your team) are not merely technical instructions. They are **strategic assets** that reflect unique domain knowledge, problem-solving logic, and proprietary process structures.

   Just as source code or trade secrets provide a competitive edge, carefully crafted AI prompts, chat builds, coded skills, and workflows, especially those developed iteratively to solve industry-specific challenges, are worthy of legal and operational protection. Organizations should consider classifying such assets under internal IP policies, leveraging trade secret law, confidentiality agreements, and access controls to guard against unauthorized disclosure or misuse.

Example: A financial services firm develops a series of proprietary prompts and decision-tree workflows for analyzing market risks using a large language model. These prompts are a blend of regulatory interpretation, firm-specific data, and trading heuristics. Trade secret protections are applied to the prompts, with access limited to a small core group within the risk and compliance team, and the company applies digital rights management tools to monitor usage and to prevent unauthorized sharing.

Reflective question: To what extent should businesses create internal registries or repositories of high-value prompts, and how can these be governed like other forms of proprietary knowledge?

2. **Train staff to structure inputs that align with IP and compliance standards.**

AI systems respond to the specificity, structure, and framing of human-generated inputs. This introduces a strategic imperative: organizations must actively train staff in how to design inputs (prompts, queries, frameworks) that not only generate optimal outputs but also conform to intellectual property (IP), privacy, and compliance obligations. For instance, prompts should avoid inadvertently including third-party confidential information or copyrighted materials unless it can be shown that they were properly licensed or authorized to be used.

Moreover, inputs that direct AI to generate patentable inventions or copyrightable expressions must be documented and attributable. Training programs for AI use should include guidance on both the legal restrictions to be aware of and technical prompt construction to educate the workforce on both the creative and regulatory aspects of AI use.

Example: A global marketing agency provides prompt engineering training to its creative teams. The sessions cover not only how to elicit branded content from AI tools but also how to avoid using client-confidential taglines or competitor trademarks in prompts. Staff are also taught to flag outputs that may trigger copyright concerns and to log their inputs in a shared IP and trademark compliance portal.

Reflective question: What kinds of internal guidelines or training modules are needed to help teams generate prompts that are both effective and legally sound?

3. **Monitor revision history and decision pathways to support claims of human authorship or co-authorship when needed.**

   Determining authorship when content is co-created with AI is a complex question. To substantiate claims of human authorship or joint authorship, organizations must proactively preserve metadata, revision histories, prompt sequences, and decision pathways that document the creative contributions of humans throughout the development process.

This documentation is not just evidence for ownership claims; it can also inform ethical use policies, ensure regulatory compliance, and strengthen commercial assertions over the resulting outputs. Digital technologies such as prompt logging, versioning systems, and digital provenance tools can play a critical role in this effort.

The US Copyright Office published a report in January 2025, "Copyright and Artificial Intelligence," which speaks to the assistance provided by AI tools and how outputs from prompts may or may not provide the basis for copyright. "The Office concludes that, given current generally available technology, prompts alone do not provide sufficient human control to make users of an AI system the authors of the output" (page 18).

Example: A software company using AI to draft code includes integrated logging that records each user's prompts and any manual edits made to the output. When seeking copyright registration for a particular software module, the company includes this log as evidence of substantial human authorship. This proves pivotal in a dispute where a competitor questions the originality and ownership of the code.

Reflective question: What systems can be implemented to catalogue and support the human decision-making inputs that shape AI-generated content? Does your company need copyright protection and thus should require control of AI use that could negate access to that protection?

Acting on these three areas alone will make a significant difference in the level of IP protection your company wields over your AI-supported innovations.

Data As a Proprietary Asset

Everything AI does either:

1. Uses IP or
2. Creates prospective IP

Accordingly, thinking about processes, policies, and ownership of AI should be at the forefront of managing risk and opportunities as mission central to the usage of AI in any business. Further, every use of AI could be potentially discoverable in any litigation, but particularly IP-based litigation. Accordingly, considering not just the policies or checklists but the strategic processes and organizational structure needed for the future is essential.

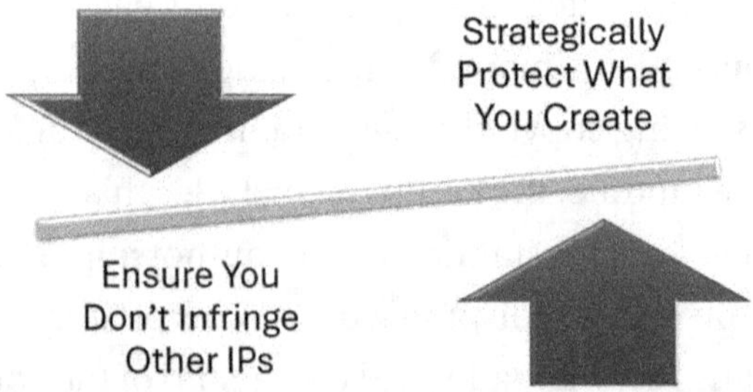

Historically, companies have taken time to evaluate how and whether to protect their innovations and often have waited to seek IP when a product is ready for market. Savvy companies have evolved to strategically build IP proactively, but as the ability to create becomes easier and the barrier to entry to do so lessens, more companies will need to consider where and how IP asset creation fits into their development cycle. When

AI is used, it cannot be an afterthought, but rather must be carefully considered earlier in the development lifecycle. This means companies may need to rethink how IP expertise integrates into the process and/or placing an AI/IP expert into the development team.

As AI systems become increasingly reliant on vast datasets to train models, the merging of IP law and AI training practices has become both complex and critical. The underlying question is: who owns the rights to the information that makes AI "intelligent"? This question has been at the forefront of much of the thought leadership on AI and IP in these early years. As it evolves, the need for continuous process improvement will also be needed. In Chapter 4, we'll cover more on the processes and governance that are needed to implement effective AI IP policies.

Protection of Training Datasets Under IP Law

The datasets used to train AI systems may be protected under existing IP laws and policy, depending on how the data is compiled, curated, and structured. While raw data is generally not copyrightable in the United States, the selection, coordination, or arrangement of data can be protected as a "compilation" under copyright law if it meets the threshold of originality. For example, a database of annotated images or a curated text corpus could potentially qualify for copyright protection. Additionally, datasets that include proprietary information, trade secrets, or confidential business data may be protected under trade secret law, assuming reasonable steps are taken to maintain their secrecy. Companies compiling training data should use access controls, non-disclosure agreements, and robust licensing frameworks to reinforce their ownership rights and deter unauthorized use.

Fair Use and the Limits of Training on Copyrighted Material

Training AI systems on copyrighted works without permission raises questions about fair use, particularly when the original works are scraped or ingested at scale without compensation to the creators. Courts have not yet settled this issue definitively, but the fair use doctrine, particularly in the United States, may provide limited cover when the use is deemed "transformative," non-commercial, and minimally harmful to the market for the original work. However, mass ingestion of copyrighted content (e.g., books, images, music) into generative AI systems could fall outside fair use when it substitutes for or competes with the original works or when the use is not sufficiently transformative.

This is not unlike lawsuits from decades ago as the internet introduced new ways to scrape content from other websites to use for commercial purposes. Several landmark cases have shaped how US courts view web scraping.

- In **eBay v. Bidder's Edge**, a court treated bot-based scraping as a trespass to chattels because it burdened eBay's servers, setting an early precedent even outside copyright law.
- **Facebook v. Power Ventures** affirmed that violating a site's terms of service and bypassing IP blocks can trigger liability under the Computer Fraud and Abuse Act (CFAA) and state anti-hacking laws.
- **Associated Press v. Meltwater** made clear that scraping and reselling news snippets for commercial use is not fair use and can constitute copyright infringement.

Together, these cases show that unauthorized scraping can violate property rights, terms of service, anti-hacking statutes, and copyright law, especially in commercial contexts or when technical barriers are bypassed. Some cases distinguished public data scraping as not inherently unlawful, especially where copyright or Computer Fraud and Abuse Act violations are not clearly established. However, scraping private, copyrighted, or commercially valuable content, especially when violating a site's terms or evading technical barriers, can lead to serious liability. These long-standing cases and interpretation can provide guidance in making strategic decisions about use of protected content when building and using AI tools.

It is a reasonable assumption that using copyrightable works in AI training could be compared to scraping and is worthy of more exploration in future policy development.

Addressing Potential Infringements in AI Training

For companies and creators, proactively addressing potential IP infringement in AI training requires a multi-layered strategy.

First, organizations developing AI systems should vet their training data sources and secure licenses where feasible, especially when data includes copyrighted, proprietary, or confidential content.

Second, creators whose works are used without consent may seek remedies through takedown notices, licensing negotiations, or litigation, depending on the jurisdiction. There is also a growing call for regulatory and industry-led frameworks that require disclosure of training data sources and allow rights holders to opt out of having their works used in AI training. Some jurisdictions, such as the EU, are beginning to implement such transparency requirements under their AI Act and Digital Services Act. In the meantime, ethical use of training data should be a cornerstone of AI development, with companies adopting clear internal policies on data acquisition, fair use boundaries, and response mechanisms when infringement claims arise.

Ultimately, the question is not whether AI will continue to learn from human-created works, but rather how the law, ethics, and innovation process will coexist in this evolving landscape. Undoubtedly, lawsuits will come in the years ahead, creating case law and precedent to drive more refined decision-making.

Early on in this process, there have been well-publicized licensing deals between publishing companies and AI firms recognizing the shift from lawsuits to monetization strategies and the acceptance that AI companies will need to license content to freely train. This represents an acceleration of the process from the early days of the internet.

Major publishers are increasingly shifting from litigation to monetization by licensing their content to AI developers. News and media organizations like *The New York Times*, Condé Nast, Hearst, the Associated Press, Axel Springer, *Le Monde*, PRISA, and the *Financial Times* have struck multi-year deals with companies such as Amazon, OpenAI, Google, and Meta. These agreements range from training large language models to providing real-time feeds, summaries, and specialized editorial content, with some commanding multi-million-dollar annual payments.

Academic and scholarly publishers are capitalizing on the demand for high-quality training material, generating tens of millions in revenue. Book publishers are experimenting with per-title fee models, as seen in HarperCollins' initiative with built-in revenue sharing for authors. Licensing collectives are pioneering blanket agreements that distribute pooled funds to rights holders.

Overall, these deals signal the emergence of a structured market where AI companies pay for premium, rights-cleared content, blending attribution, revenue sharing, and access terms to address legal risk and secure long-term partnerships.

Boundaries of Fair Use in AI Training

The application of the fair use doctrine to AI training remains one of the most hotly contested and unsettled areas in copyright law. US courts evaluate fair use under the four-factor test outlined in 17 U.S.C. § 107:

1. Considering the purpose and character of the use
2. The nature of the copyrighted work
3. The amount used
4. The effect of the use on the potential market for the original

In Authors Guild v. Google, Inc., 804 F.3d 202 (2d Cir. 2015), the Second Circuit held that Google's digitization of books for a searchable index constituted transformative fair use, in part because it did not replace the market for the original works. This decision is often cited as an early precedent supporting the argument that large-scale data may qualify as fair use.

However, current litigation is testing whether that logic applies to generative AI. In Andersen v. Stability AI Ltd., artists alleged that AI companies used their copyrighted images to train models like Stable Diffusion without consent, potentially exceeding the bounds of fair use by creating derivative works. Similarly, Doe v. GitHub, Inc., challenges GitHub Copilot's training on open-source code without attribution, raising issues of license compliance and copyright infringement.

As these cases develop, they will clarify whether training AI models on copyrighted material without permission is considered transformative and thus defensible under fair use or if it constitutes infringement that requires licensing.

To mitigate the risk of infringement, companies training AI models must adopt proactive and layered strategies. This includes prioritizing the use of public domain and openly licensed datasets, obtaining licenses for proprietary content, and maintaining robust documentation to support the provenance and legality of training data. At the time of publication with AI assisted research, below are a few of the notable cases on this issue in progress.

Case	Jurisdiction	Issue	Current Status
Bartz v. Anthropic	N.D. Cal.	Books used to train Claude	Court held that training on books was fair use, but Anthropic infringed by keeping a central library of pirated books; later, the court preliminarily approved a **$1.5 B class settlement**. Case now in settlement administration.
Kadrey v. Meta	N.D. Cal.	Books used to train Llama	Court granted summary judgment for Meta – training = fair use (no shown market harm); some non-training/distribution claims continue.
Thomson Reuters v. ROSS Intelligence	D. Del.	Use of Westlaw headnotes to train a legal AI	The court (February 11, 2025) rejected the fair use defense for ROSS's copying of headnotes, finding the use was not fair use; case is on appeal.

(continued)

Case	Jurisdiction	Issue	Current Status
The New York Times v. OpenAI & Microsoft	S.D.N.Y.	Use of news articles to train models	The court allowed the core copyright claims to proceed; the case is now in discovery.
The Intercept v. OpenAI	S.D.N.Y.	Use of news articles to train ChatGPT; DMCA/ copyright claims	The judge allowed parts of the suit to proceed (notably a claim over removal of copyright-management info), while dismissing other claims.
Microsoft – Authors' lawsuit	S.D.N.Y.	Alleged use of ~200,000 pirated books to train "Megatron"	Filed June, 2025; currently at the pleading stage, no substantive rulings yet.
Apple – Authors' lawsuit (Apple Intelligence)	N.D. Cal.	Alleged use of pirated books for training	Filed October, 2025; newly filed, no substantive rulings yet.
Salesforce – Authors' lawsuit (xGen)	N.D. Cal.	Alleged use of copyrighted books for training	Filed October, 2025; newly filed, no substantive rulings yet.

Infringement Detection and Liability

How Can AI Tools Be Used to Identify IP Infringement More Effectively?

AI tools can significantly enhance the ability to identify potential intellectual property (IP) infringement by automating and accelerating detection processes that would otherwise require extensive manual review. Some key applications include

1. **Content scanning and similarity detection**: AI-powered image, text, and audio recognition tools can compare new content against massive databases of copyrighted or trademarked material to identify similarities. For example, machine learning algorithms can detect near-duplicate text, plagiarized writing, or reused code, even if it's been modified or rephrased.

2. **Trademark monitoring**: Natural language processing (NLP) and image recognition tools can continuously scan domain names, ecommerce platforms, social media, and app stores for unauthorized use of brand names, logos, or product images. This helps brand owners detect counterfeit goods or infringing use of marks more quickly than traditional methods.

3. **Copyright violation detection in digital media**: AI can be used to analyze videos, songs, and images uploaded to platforms in real time. YouTube's Content ID system is an early example, but more advanced systems can identify background music, artwork, or even style mimicry that may raise infringement concerns.

4. **Patent similarity search**: AI tools trained on patent databases can evaluate invention disclosures and claims to determine whether they overlap with existing patents, helping inventors avoid unintentional infringement and enabling legal teams to better assess freedom to operate or patentability.
5. **Automated alerts and enforcement tools**: AI can not only identify potential infringement but also trigger automated alerts or even initiate takedown notices. This improves response times and allows companies to scale enforcement efforts.

As AI continues to evolve, it can serve not only as a detection mechanism but also as a risk prediction engine, flagging likely problem areas in contracts, code, content, or creative works before they are published or commercialized.

A growing ecosystem of AI-enabled tools is emerging to help organizations protect intellectual property as generative technologies accelerate the creation and circulation of digital content. Several platforms focus on detecting unauthorized use or copying:

- Copyleaks and authorship verification tools like Turnitin and Originality.ai analyze text to determine whether it was produced by AI and whether it infringes existing copyrighted materials.
- AllSearch.ai and similar reverse image search tools trace visual content back to original assets, helping creators verify originality and enforce rights.

- Deepfake detection technologies such as Amber Video and Deepware Scanner protect individuals and brands from unauthorized use of likeness or identity in synthetic media.
- Meanwhile, Imatag provides invisible watermarking to track images in AI training and output, enabling detection of misuse long after content is published.

Other tools focus on active rights control, licensing, and monitoring. Pex and Smart Protection help rights holders track and enforce copyright across music, images, video, and text, including in AI-generated derivatives and content marketplaces. RightHub integrates licensing and rights management directly into AI workflows to prevent unlicensed source material from being used in development. The Getty Images–Bria.ai partnership represents an emerging model in which licensing terms are embedded into AI systems themselves to ensure responsible use. Together, these tools illustrate how watermarking, detection, licensing, and attribution technologies are converging to form a layered IP compliance infrastructure for the AI era.

Who Is Liable When AI Inadvertently Generates Content That Infringes on Existing IP?

The question of liability for AI-generated infringement remains unsettled in many jurisdictions, but several emerging principles are guiding the discussion:

1. **Human accountability prevails**: Current legal frameworks place responsibility on the human or corporate actor that owns, deploys, or benefits from the AI tool. Courts have generally declined to treat AI as a legal entity capable of liability. Therefore,

if an AI tool generates infringing content, such as plagiarized text, derivative art, or infringing music, the liability typically falls on the person or organization that operated or published the AI-generated work.

2. **The role of developers and providers**: In some cases, liability may extend to the developers or providers of the AI system, particularly if they failed to implement adequate safeguards or trained their models on copyrighted material without permission. For instance, lawsuits against generative AI companies like OpenAI, Stability AI, and GitHub Copilot have questioned whether the companies should be held liable for training on protected content without licenses.

3. **Contributory or vicarious infringement**: If a platform knowingly enables users to generate infringing content and benefits financially, it may be liable under theories of contributory or vicarious infringement. This is especially relevant in commercial settings where the platform profits from widespread use of infringing outputs.

4. **User responsibility and licensing risks**: The party who publishes or uses the AI-generated content commercially may bear the final liability, particularly if they failed to perform due diligence or relied on AI-generated work without verifying originality. Contractual terms and AI tool licenses often include disclaimers that shift responsibility to the user.

While AI may be the tool that produces the infringing material, legal responsibility remains squarely on the humans and companies that use, train, and distribute the content. As AI usage scales, developing clear accountability frameworks and audit trails will be essential to manage risk and ensure compliance with IP laws.

Patents and AI Innovation

A company may rightfully wonder whether any of the new workflows they develop using AI can be protected as a competitive advantage. In many cases, yes, the use of AI can be a patentable invention. How do we know this? Because we can see the evidence of it in granted patents. The invention must still meet the basic requirements for the United States Patent and Trademark Office (USPTO), which include new, useful, and non-obvious (per legal definitions). There do exist particular challenges to patenting software-based inventions. Below we describe the current AI patent landscape at a very high level, what the threshold is for meeting operability requirements of AI/software patents, and some predictions (and concerns) as to where the space is headed in terms of IP protection.

In order to provide some patent data, a few definitions and boundary conditions needed to be selected. In this case, we collected data on active granted and pending patents, in the United States, from 2006 to the present. To confine the millions of patents to the correct technology space, we used "patent classification codes," which are used to assign inventions to chosen groups within the USPTO for review (called the examination process). All the patents under that code should belong to the same technology area. It is a rough-cut approach to view patent activity in a target technology space.

There exist many more detailed ways to study patent trends with higher fidelity; however, for general trends this is an acceptable approach. For this analysis, patent filings were not human-screened for relevancy to the AI space; the data was obtained and analyzed electronically.

For this study, the following classification codes were used to limit the dataset:

- **USPC Class 706: Data Processing — Artificial Intelligence**
  - **General definition**: Class 706 covers digital data processing systems and methods for emulating intelligence. This includes knowledge-based systems, reasoning systems, knowledge acquisition systems, and systems for reasoning with uncertainty (e.g., fuzzy logic systems), adaptive systems, machine learning systems, and artificial neural networks (USPTO).
- **CPC Subclass G06N: Computing Arrangements Based on Specific Computational Models**
  - **General definition**: Subclass G06N covers computing arrangements based on specific computational models, such as artificial intelligence models, neural networks, and machine learning techniques. It includes systems that simulate or emulate cognitive functions, learning methods, and reasoning processes (USPTO).

Under these two patent classifications, from 2006 to the present, **144,156 patent filings were made**. Still think that AI is unpatentable? This figure is highly inclusive of all types of AI, ranging from neural networks, supervised and unsupervised learning, to fuzzy logic and other AI techniques. But the point is that AI has been part of patentable inventions for quite a long time.

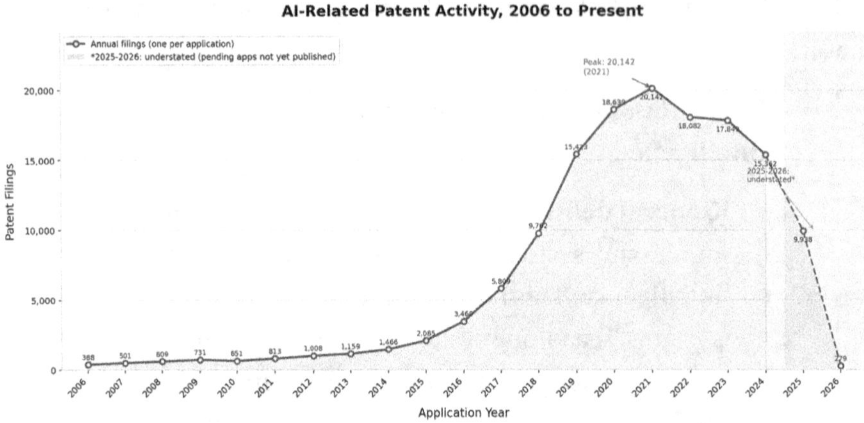

[Note: The number of patent filings for 2024 through 2026 represent incomplete data, due to the 18-month publication window when patent applications are first laid open.]

Clearly the rate and number of patent applications began climbing after 2015 and dramatically accelerates between 2017 and 2021. Some possible milestone events that may have contributed to the increase include:

- Significant advancements in areas including deep learning and neural network that began appearing in 2015–2017 such as Microsoft's speech recognition system based on deep learning foundations.
- Google introduced the "Transformer" architecture in 2017, advancing machine translation using "attention mechanism" within machine learning.
- In 2018, NVIDIA introduced GPU innovations to enable training of AI models, including the Pascal, Volta, Tesla, and Turing GPU architectures.
- Cloud AI platforms like AWS SageMaker and Azure ML began to spread the availability of AI use in 2017.

- Open-source machine learning, such as TensorFlow, became available in 2015. There are many other launches and continued new tools and services that have continued to refresh and advance the AI landscape.

The technical innovations, paired with widespread availability of tools, and more easily accessible computing power provided companies with ways to solve problems and create products with an innovative twist. Examples include AI diagnostics in healthcare, predictive maintenance in manufacturing, recommendation engines in retail, and automation and risk assessment in legal/financial services. All of these advancements lead to potentially patentable inventions, which many companies have pursued over the past 20 years.

Now let's look at the companies that own the most patents in these patent classifications, again from 2006 to the present. IBM is far and away the leader in the space. Familiar tech companies including Google, Samsung, Microsoft, and Amazon are in the top six patent holders. Computer and chip manufacturers are also present, including Intel, Qualcomm, and Dell. Even selected financial services companies Capital One and Bank of America appear in the top assignees.

What do these patents look like? It may be surprising to learn that there are very practical uses of AI being patented and it isn't limited to highly esoteric mathematical solutions.

Bank of America, who appears in the second half of the pack of top assignees, issued a press release in October 2024 that cited a 94% increase in AI patents since 2022, and, "Today, the company has nearly 1,100 AI and ML patents and pending applications in its portfolio, with more than half having already been granted."

Bank of America further notes that they have 76 active patent filings on their virtual financial assistant "Erica," a feature that many bank customers are familiar with.

Does this mean that there is no more room for AI patents? Not at all. Recall that these patent classification codes cover a wide variety of AI approaches, so an individual approach, for a specific purpose, may still qualify as a patentable invention. Over time, patents in a given technology space begin to become more specific and narrower once the foundational, broad patents have been granted. But these more targeted patents can still be invaluable to a company to help protect their products and services.

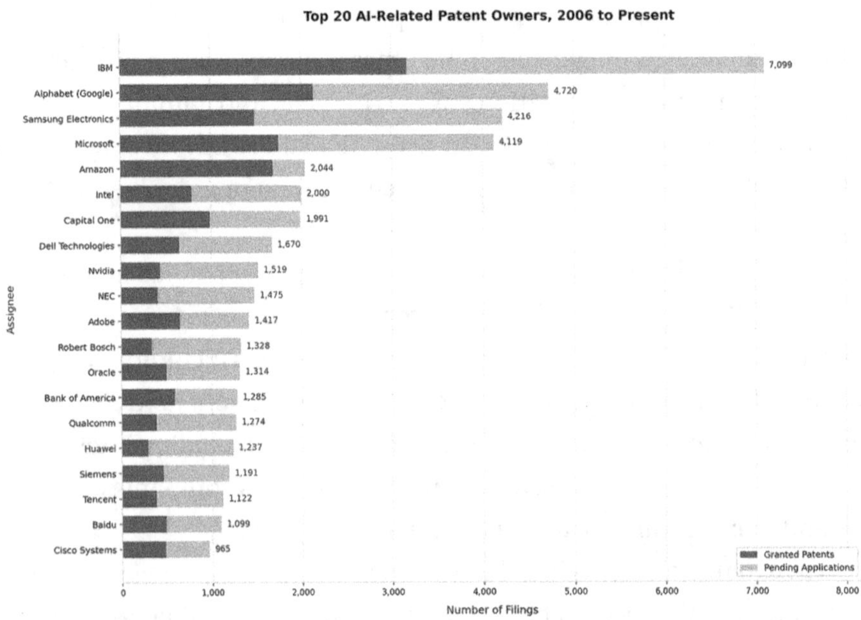

It should be noted that another protection route is to keep AI processes as confidential information or even more robustly guarded as a trade secret. So even if AI-supported tools and workflows do not appear to be patentable, there are ways to protect a company's valued AI information without patents. A trade secret program helps to establish protocol with employees and also provides the legal basis required to allow enforcement of trade secret misappropriation. If such a program does not exist, the company risks heavy losses of proprietary information through employee attrition, inadvertent sharing of proprietary information, or malicious theft. With widespread uses of AI within companies, loss of valuable information becomes incredibly likely in the absence of policies and active management.

What does the future hold for AI patents? We may have witnessed an interim peak in patenting, with a decreased rate of patents to follow based on the core areas that provided so many patents in the last ten years in the AI patent landscape. However, that trend could easily become renewed with the addition of new technological advancements that in turn provide new innovation "fuel" to create new patents.

Those technologies may include topics such as highly specialized combinations of hardware and software for AI use, as new AI-focused chip sets are introduced by companies such as NVIDIA. Quantum computing, once full scale and commercialized, is also a future frontier that will likely provide new patent opportunities in conjunction with AI. Sophisticated "simulated worlds" or digital twins using AI may provide new patentable concepts. Finally, neuromorphic (brain-mimicking) chips contribute to the path toward AI superintelligence and will also likely provide innovations that lead to patents.

Policy Preview

Clear policies are only the starting line. Written standards can outline expectations, but without defined processes, accountable structures, and implementation plans, they rarely change behavior or meaningfully reduce risk. For AI-driven work, in particular, compliance cannot rely on employee interpretation or after-the-fact review. The company must embed IP safeguards into workflows, procurement steps, vendor management, product design, and human review cycles. Roles and responsibilities need to be assigned, technology tools must support enforcement, and audit trails must be easy to maintain. Just as important, cross-functional coordination among legal, IT, R&D, product, compliance, and business units ensures that approved tools, training data, contracting protocols, and attribution practices are consistently applied. A policy sets the guardrails, but only structure, process, and operational discipline will translate those rules into reduced exposure and sustainable IP asset growth. We have provided sample policies online at `www.owning-intelligence.com`. The following areas are just a few that require policy and process:

- The use of AI tools that generate content (e.g., text, code, images, audio, video)
- The use of datasets to train or fine-tune AI models
- The commercial use or publication of AI-generated outputs
- The procurement of third-party AI tools or services
- Legal obligations under copyright, patent, trademark, and trade secret law

The coming chapters will dig deeper into governance, policies, where AI governance and compliance should reside, and a roadmap for leaders to consider.

Key Takeaways

- Distinguish AI-generated from AI-assisted works, because authorship, registrability, and ownership turn on the degree of human creative control.
- Treat data as a proprietary asset: Curate, license, and document training and prompt data, and protect sensitive inputs under trade secret regimes.
- Fair use for training is unsettled; outcomes will hinge on transformation, market effects, and provenance, with active litigation shaping the boundaries.

- Build employee AI policies now: Approved tools, prohibited uses, prompt hygiene, fact-checking, and mandatory human review before any external release.
- Capture inventiveness: When AI supports R&D, log prompts, sources, and revisions to preserve patentability and evidentiary trails.
- Operationalize "work for hire" for AI: Update employee IP assignments and vendor contracts so AI-assisted outputs are clearly owned, licensed, and indemnified.
- Strengthen third-party terms: Require data provenance disclosures, IP warranties, indemnities, and explicit restrictions on model reuse of your data.
- Treat high-value prompts and workflows as trade secrets, with access controls, NDAs, registries, and usage monitoring.
- Maintain attribution: Keep version histories, prompt logs, and decision records to substantiate human authorship and manage audit and compliance.
- Use layered detection: Combine plagiarism, reverse-image, deepfake, and watermarking tools to find and remediate infringement in AI outputs.
- Assign accountability: Legal responsibility sits with humans and organizations that deploy, publish, and profit from AI outputs, not with the AI system.
- Prefer licensed, public domain, or openly licensed datasets; where proprietary content is used, obtain licenses and document scope and terms.

- Monitor regulatory trends: EU transparency and opt-out regimes, and US case law on scraping and fair use, will influence training data practices.
- Leverage patents where appropriate: AI-enabled inventions can be patentable; activity shows room for focused, domain-specific claims.
- Use trade secrets as a parallel strategy when patents are impractical, and implement a robust secrecy program to avoid accidental leakage.
- Expect a shift from lawsuits to licensing: Publishers and platforms are striking content deals with AI firms that blend attribution, revenue share, and risk controls.
- Embed IP controls into product and procurement lifecycles, including approval gates, automated scans, and cross-functional sign-offs.
- Prepare incident response: Define takedown, rollback, and remediation steps for suspected infringement, with rapid legal notification paths.
- Measure and audit: Set key performance indicators (KPIs) for tool usage, approval compliance, and dataset provenance; run periodic audits to enforce the policy.
- Bottom line: Policy is the guardrail, but process, structure, contracts, and disciplined implementation are what actually reduce risk and grow IP assets.

CHAPTER 4

Oversight and Accountability

How boards, executives, and legal teams must prepare for AI accountability, compliance, and oversight

As data and use of AI to build intellectual assets become more mission critical to organizations, strong governance, processes, and oversight have never been more essential. Algorithms become co-creators and decision-makers in innovation such that the lines between human- and machine-generated IPs are blurring, ushering in complex legal, ethical, and operational challenges.

Without thoughtful governance frameworks and risk-aware oversight, organizations risk not only losing control of their most valuable intangible assets but also exposing themselves to liability, infringement, regulatory scrutiny, and reputational harm. This is not a one and done. Governance will be driven by leadership and the board, but implemented across the organization and provide an ongoing monitoring and support system. A few of the governance categories needed include the following:

J. C. Wolfe and N. E. Cronin, *Owning Intelligence*,
https://doi.org/10.1007/979-8-8688-2388-6_4

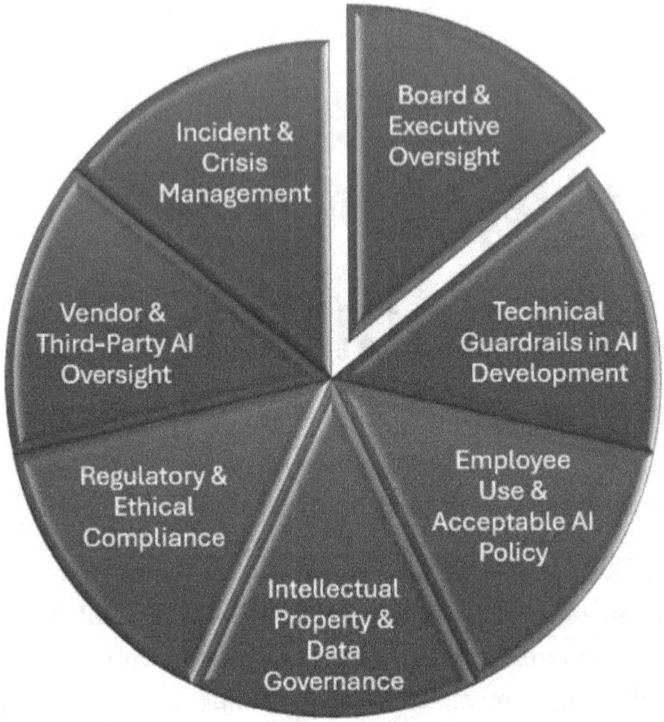

Board and Executive Oversight

AI governance starts at the top, where boards and executive leaders determine how AI supports the organization's mission, risk appetite, and strategic goals. Their role includes setting accountability structures, approving investments, and ensuring that oversight mechanisms exist across functions. Without senior-level ownership, AI initiatives risk becoming fragmented, under-supervised, or misaligned with broader business priorities. As budgets remain tight, prioritization and allocation of resources is a board level responsibility.

Technical Guardrails in AI Development

Guardrails built into the development lifecycle protect against biased outputs, security flaws, and unsafe deployment. This includes rigorous testing, red-teaming, human-in-the-loop design and crisis identification, model explainability measures, and secure data architectures. Technical standards and checkpoints ensure AI systems are monitored continuously and can be audited or deactivated when risks emerge. Further, processes are needed to ensure if a threat to safety is probable, that appropriate measures to respond ethically and responsibly.

Employee Use and Acceptable AI Policy
Clear internal policies define when, how, and by whom AI tools may be used. These policies guide employees on confidentiality, data input restrictions, decision-making boundaries, and accountability. Training and enforcement are essential to reduce legal, ethical, and operational risks while empowering employees to use AI responsibly and productively. Keep in mind, the policies are just a written statement. The process, culture, incentives and accountability are what ensure effective implementation.

Intellectual Property and Data Governance
Owning and protecting data and AI outputs is central to long-term value and legal compliance. Governance must clarify data sourcing, licensing, model training rights, and ownership of generative outputs. Safeguards around trade secrets, proprietary datasets, and AI-enabled inventions ensure both innovation and defensibility in a rapidly evolving legal landscape.

Regulatory and Ethical Compliance
Organizations face expanding obligations from sector-specific rules, data protection laws, and emerging AI regulations. Ethical standards, such as transparency, fairness, privacy, and accountability, complement legal requirements. Proactive monitoring, compliance audits, and documentation practices help anticipate regulatory shifts and demonstrate responsible stewardship.

Vendor and Third-Party AI Oversight

AI systems rarely exist in isolation, making vendor relationships a critical oversight area. Due diligence, contractual controls, audit rights, and visibility into model development and data practices help manage external risk. Organizations must apply the same standards to third-party tools and services that they apply internally.

Incident and Crisis Management

Even well-governed AI systems can fail or cause harm, making preparedness essential. Crisis plans should cover detection, escalation protocols, legal review, stakeholder communication, remediation steps, and post-incident analysis. A structured response framework limits damage, preserves trust, and strengthens future risk mitigation efforts.

A sample of these policies can be found online at `www.owning-intelligence.com`. But beyond these broad categories, boards must consider the impact areas to ensure policies encompass the wide array of risk exposure points. This is just one of many constructs and approaches to managing such a fluid and rapidly changing area.

Operational governance by cross-functional teams with checks and balances requires policies and processes with audits by disinterested third parties. Likewise, as will be covered more in this chapter, governance starts at the top with the board of directors ultimately responsible for ensuring that the necessary policies, incentives, benchmarks, and safeguards are put in place and followed.

Policies are surely important and AI can help write and create policies. Tools driven by AI can assist in tracking. But policies must be implemented largely by humans or minimally monitored by humans, at least in the foreseeable future. Somewhere in the governance process and liability spectrum is a need for humans to follow the policies and ensure compliance with the policies.

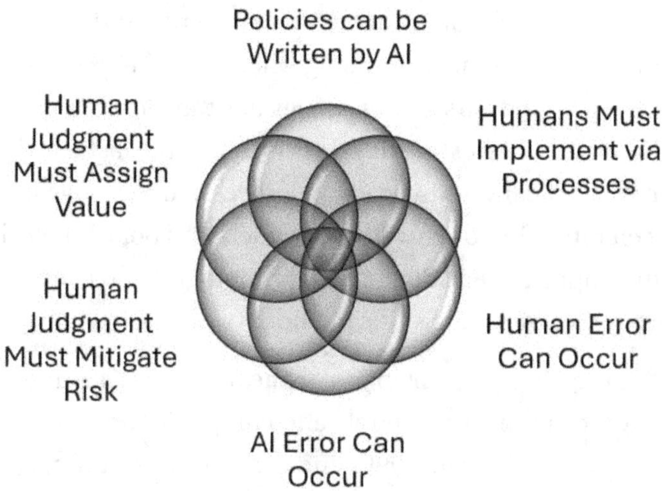

As that becomes increasingly difficult, entire management functions may be focused on compliance. Everywhere humans interact with AI in this new system will be potential jobs of the future. This chapter focuses on areas that will need governance and the processes that may be necessary to manage risk going forward.

Companies like Google and Microsoft, the National Institute of Standards and Technology (NIST), universities, professional associations, and more are crafting policies and best practices designed to build in guardrails against these issues. The creators of AI are focused on these categories of risk, but in the near future, every organization will need to understand and build in their own guardrails for the implementation using these AI tools.

Before mapping out a structure for such a complex governance model, it's helpful to look at past historical shifts of this magnitude to draw parallels where appropriate and learn from past mistakes to make the best possible decisions going forward. To plan for an unknown future, we must build reasonable assumptions from past experiences.

The evolution of technology demanding governance is not new. We could spend countless hours discussing what worked and what went wrong over the past 30 years as technology has transformed the need for oversight. What's interesting to assess is that in the last few decades, governance was typically a slow-moving process. In recent years, there has been an acceleration in how governing models and boards have begun to recognize the importance of disruptive technologies and cybersecurity.

A few examples of the big shifts include:

- The creation of the Domain Name System (DNS) and internet connecting people and companies around the globe in the late 1990s and early 2000s, resulting in the explosion of online commerce or connectivity, breaking down barriers in business and culture
- The subsequent adoption and widespread use of open-source code in the early 2000s and beyond to allow for scaled and rapid growth
- The proliferation of cybersecurity events and threats to every organization over the last 25 years, which is now exacerbated by deep fakes and the use of AI by bad actors
- The introduction of smartphones and social media into our culture often infringing on privacy and building a treasure trove of data that company seek to use
- The fundamental business model of leveraging data and regulation of privacy
- Finally, leading to today as we tackle the governance of artificial intelligence

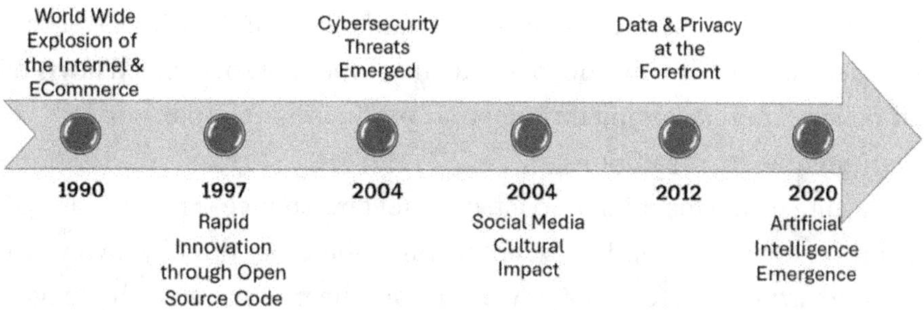

The Internet

In the 1990s, as commercial interest in domain names surged and internet usage entered the mainstream, it became increasingly clear that standardization and governance mechanisms were essential. Initially, the Domain Name System (DNS) was managed by the U.S. Department of Defense, but in 1992, operational responsibility was subcontracted to Network Solutions, Inc (Network Solutions). The National Science Foundation (NSF) later assumed the funding role, engaging Network Solutions to oversee domain name registration for most top-level domains under a five-year agreement. By 1998, authority was transferred to the U.S. Department of Commerce. Around this time, an international coalition led by Jon Postel came together to establish the Internet Corporation for Assigned Names and Numbers (ICANN), defining its governance principles and bylaws. With ICANN's formation in 1998, the foundational structure of internet governance took shape, including the formal separation of registrars (e.g., GoDaddy) and registry operators (e.g., Verisign, Managing.com). Notably, any changes to the root zone of the internet required US government approval, a control that remained in place until 2016, when the Obama administration transitioned oversight to the global community.

In parallel, the Internet Engineering Task Force (IETF) emerged as a voluntary, non-commercial consortium of individuals focused on the technical development and operation of the internet's architecture. While participation in the IETF is open, it is primarily composed of technologists from academia, infrastructure providers, and related industries. Over time, the governance of the internet became the domain of specialized lawyers and policy experts working through non-profit, international, non-governmental organizations.

Despite its far-reaching impact, internet governance is rarely featured on corporate board agendas, except within companies directly involved in its infrastructure. However, as we confront the multifaceted challenges of artificial intelligence deployment, examining how the internet's governance framework evolved may offer valuable lessons for shaping effective AI policy. Will a similar global organization emerge? Will the United States lead in building that model as it did before? Will stakeholders be identified and incorporated structurally into a governing body? Going forward, as these new AI governance organizations emerge, what will your company's role be in its creation? Will you be a leader, a participant, or merely an observer?

The Introduction of Open-Source Code

In the early 2000s, companies began adopting open-source code not only as a cost-saving measure but as a strategic asset. What began as a grassroots, developer-driven movement quickly became a foundational element of enterprise software development. Industry leaders such as IBM, Google, and Red Hat invested significantly in open-source communities. This shift enabled organizations to accelerate innovation, avoid vendor lock-in, and build more secure, customizable systems. Over time, open source evolved from a fringe concept into a mainstream practice, fundamentally reshaping the software industry and laying the groundwork for today's collaborative, cloud-native environments.

However, the widespread use of open-source code also introduced new cybersecurity risks. Many companies initially relegated these concerns to the IT department, but major breaches, often caused by failure to patch known vulnerabilities in open-source components, elevated the issue to senior leadership and even board-level discussions. Most notable, Equifax, the keeper of our most valuable asset, our financial data, failed to patch a known open-source code vulnerability resulting in more than 100 million US citizens being compromised because a simple patch was not installed. Many other examples followed plaguing our most trusted industry segments including breaches at Capital One, First American, State Farm, Quest Diagnostics, and Target, among others. Despite the number of case studies, many businesses, large and small, public and private, continue to relegate open-source code compliance to IT departments without much oversight by other departments.

Cybersecurity

Forward-thinking organizations began to recognize the value of a cross-functional approach, involving legal and compliance teams to establish governance policies that support IT in managing risk. This collaborative model offers a valuable blueprint as businesses now confront similar governance challenges in the AI era.

Historically, companies approached cybersecurity risk management as a reactive IT function, often focused on firewalls, antivirus software, and basic network protections. However, as cyber threats grew more sophisticated in the 2000s, driven by data breaches, ransomware, and nation-state attacks, organizations began shifting toward a more strategic, enterprise-wide approach. Risk management evolved to include threat modeling, vulnerability assessments, and incident response planning, with frameworks like the National Institute of Standards and Technology (NIST, a US federal agency under the Department of Commerce that sets best practices for technology, cybersecurity, AI, manufacturing, and measurement science) and the International Organization for Standardization (ISO, the independent, nongovernmental global body that develops and publishes international standards across every industry) gaining traction. By the 2010s, cybersecurity became a board-level concern, integrated into governance, compliance, and business continuity planning. Today, risk management is seen as a dynamic process, critical not only to protecting assets but also to maintaining trust and regulatory compliance in an increasingly digital world. However, many boards continue to add cybersecurity to the long list of responsibilities of the audit committee. As newer risks using AI emerge, it may no longer be possible to simply pile all of this into the audit committee. New committee structures will be necessary to manage the risks going forward.

Cybersecurity governance and AI governance share several key similarities, particularly in their focus on risk management, accountability, and ethical oversight. Just as cybersecurity governance aims to protect an organization from digital threats and vulnerabilities, AI governance seeks to safeguard against risks such as bias, misuse, and ethical violations in AI systems. Both require robust frameworks for identifying and mitigating potential harms, whether through regular audits, clear accountability structures, or compliance with evolving regulations. Furthermore, in both areas, governance needs to be proactive rather than reactive, with an emphasis on continuous monitoring and adaptation to rapidly changing technology landscapes. As organizations increasingly integrate AI technologies, the governance of AI will likely mirror cybersecurity governance in its need for cross-functional collaboration, with legal, technical, and ethical considerations driving the development of effective, transparent, and responsible practices.

As executives and directors scrambled to catch up to this changing environment, individuals were rapidly changing the way they connected through social media.

Social Media

The introduction of social media into our culture in the early 2000s, with platforms like Facebook (launched in 2004), Twitter (2006), and Instagram (2010), fundamentally transformed how people communicate, consume information, and influence public discourse. Initially celebrated as tools for connectivity and self-expression, these platforms quickly evolved into major forces in marketing, politics, and public opinion. However, by the mid-2010s, significant problems emerged from concerns about mental health, online harassment, and the exploitation of user data. High-profile incidents such as the Cambridge Analytica scandal in 2018 revealed just how vulnerable user privacy and personal data were, sparking global debates around ethical data use. At the same time, cybersecurity threats intensified, with hackers using social media as a vector for phishing, impersonation, and ransomware attacks. In response, companies were forced to pivot from casual, brand-driven use of these platforms to more responsible, governance-oriented strategies. This included establishing internal social media policies, training employees on safe digital behavior, investing in threat detection systems, and adopting compliance frameworks to align with evolving regulations like the EU's General Data Protection Regulation (GDPR) in 2018 and the California Consumer Privacy Act (CCPA) in 2020. Today, responsible social media use is recognized not only as a marketing imperative but as a core aspect of corporate governance, digital risk management, and stakeholder trust. While considering the governance impact of AI, we can look to the dark side of social media for guidance, recognizing that with the introduction of deep fakes of video, voice, and other AI masking, the negative impact on our culture cannot be understated.

Data and Privacy

Companies began leveraging big data in the late 2000s and early 2010s, as advancements in cloud computing, data storage, and analytics made it possible to collect and process vast amounts of information from customers, employees, and devices. Businesses quickly realized the value of using data to drive decision-making, personalize services, predict consumer behavior, and gain competitive advantages. However, as data collection became more pervasive, often through tracking technologies, loyalty programs, and third-party integrations, privacy concerns escalated. The public and regulators began questioning how data was being collected, stored, shared, and used. As a result, data governance moved from the IT department to the forefront of enterprise risk management. Today, the protection of data privacy is recognized as a board-level responsibility, requiring directors to oversee compliance, ensure ethical data practices, and evaluate the reputational and legal risks of data misuse. Governance structures, such as privacy committees and chief data officers, are increasingly integrated into corporate strategy to ensure that the use of big data aligns with both business goals and societal expectations.

A Governance Preview of AI and IP

What distinguishes AI from these historical shifts is that, at its core, AI is powered by data and that data is owned by someone. Everything about AI is rooted in intellectual property. The models are trained in inputs that originate from identifiable sources, often protected by intellectual property rights. The algorithms used to generate insights or outputs could be themselves proprietary, and the outputs they produce may also carry ownership implications. In short, every facet of the AI lifecycle from data ingestion to model development to final output involves layers of ownership, rights, and responsibilities. This reality makes it imperative that intellectual property considerations are not treated as an afterthought, but rather as an integral component of any AI governance framework. A thoughtful, proactive approach to integrating IP into AI strategy not only mitigates legal and reputational risks but also positions organizations to fully realize the value of their innovations in a rapidly evolving digital economy. Additionally, for decades, IP has often been documented in the final phase of a linear development process, rather than integrated into the development process with cross-functional teams. The liability and responsibility of the board must always be considered as something you either invest in mitigating, insure against, or delegate and seek indemnification for. We've seen this unfold in the last few decades so the basic approach has been built, but now must be augmented to fit the changing demands of AI. We can also learn from past mistakes.

Boards can look at all risk related to AI and IP based upon the three broad-based ways to manage that risk as seen in the figure below. Every risk a board faces in the use of AI must be resolved or mitigated by investing in one of the following:

1. Internal risk mitigation strategies.
2. Insurance to cover potential liability.
3. Hire another party with appropriate indemnification in the contract.

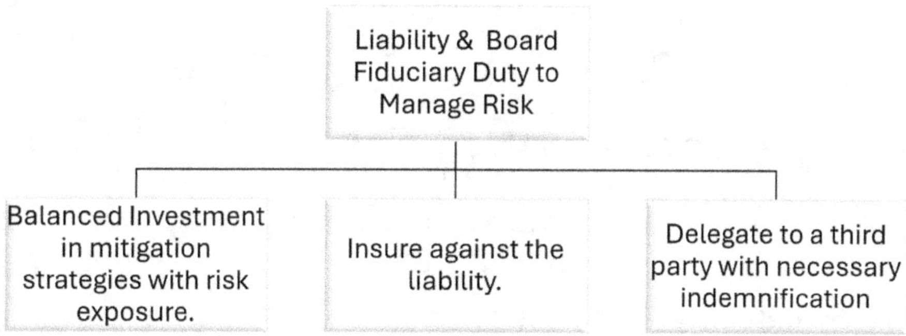

Areas of Impact: Accountability, Ethics, and Compliance Considerations

Effective AI oversight must address a wide array of issues that cut across legal, ethical, technological, and organizational domains. Below are key focus areas essential for developing responsible, secure, and inclusive AI systems.

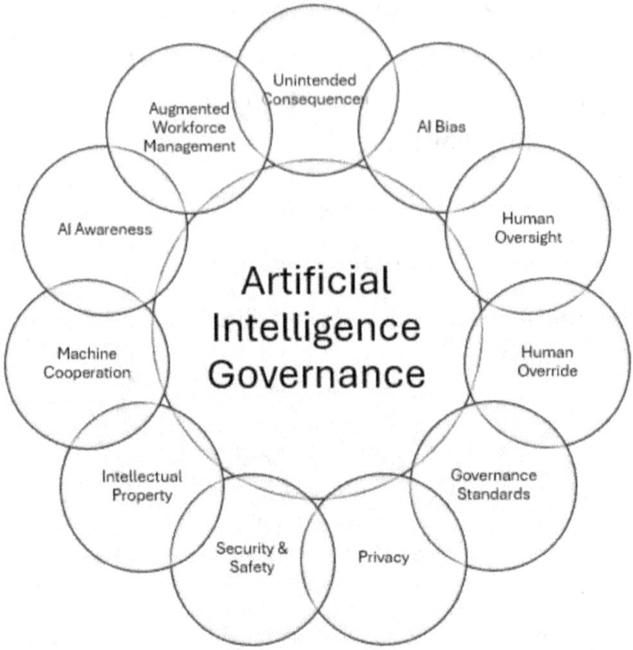

Security and Safety

AI systems must be protected from external threats and operate reliably in dynamic environments. Governance should enforce secure design principles, regular testing, and monitoring for vulnerabilities such as adversarial attacks, data poisoning, or system manipulation. Safety entails ensuring predictable and aligned outcomes, particularly in high-risk or autonomous applications, where unexpected behavior could lead to harm. Questions to ask:

- Have we identified the cybersecurity risks associated with our AI systems?
- Are our AI models protected from adversarial attacks, tampering, or data poisoning?
- What safety protocols are in place for high-risk or autonomous AI applications?

- How often are safety audits or stress tests conducted internally and by objective third parties?

Privacy

AI often relies on large datasets, many of which contain sensitive personal information. Governance must safeguard individual privacy through data minimization, anonymization, and compliance with data protection laws like the GDPR and CCPA. AI models must also be assessed for potential re-identification risks and misuse of personal data, especially in surveillance and biometric applications. Questions to ask:

- Is the data used to train and operate our AI systems compliant with privacy laws (e.g., GDPR, CCPA)?
- Are individuals informed when their data is collected, processed, or used by AI?
- Are there measures in place to anonymize or minimize personal data exposure?
- How do we manage and respond to privacy breaches related to AI?
- Are there third-party reviews?

Intellectual Property

AI raises complex questions about ownership of creative outputs, model training data, and algorithmic innovations. Governance must clarify how copyright, patent, and trade secret laws apply to AI-generated works and ensure that training data is lawfully sourced. Infringement risks must be weighed against innovation, especially in generative AI tools capable of mimicking protected works. Questions to ask:

- Who owns the outputs of our AI systems (e.g., code, designs, creative content)?
- Are we using copyrighted or proprietary data for AI training without proper licenses?

- Do we have IP protections in place for AI models or innovations we've developed?
- Are we exposed to IP infringement risks from vendors or third-party tools?
- How are we educating employees about their use of AI tools when developing written materials in the organization to protect trade secrets?
- How do we create checks and balances?
- How do we integrate strategic thinking about IP protection and creation into the innovation, development, and creative process?
- How do we build proprietary datasets for AI to use in our business?

Machine Cooperation

As AI agents increasingly interact with each other in autonomous environments, such as supply chains, financial systems, or IoT networks, governance must address inter-system trust, protocol compatibility, and conflict resolution mechanisms. Ensuring transparent cooperation between machines reduces systemic risk and improves efficiency in complex, multi-agent systems. Questions to ask:

- Are our AI systems interoperable with partners, vendors, or public infrastructure?
- Do we understand how autonomous agents interact with each other in our digital ecosystem?
- Can we ensure that agentic AI systems of others cannot access or obtain proprietary information from our systems?

- Have we assessed the risks of cascading errors or systemic vulnerabilities from interconnected AI systems?
- Who will lead in writing policies related to third parties?
- Are we involved in national or global organizations building policies related to AI? Should we be?
- Who is empowered in the organization to provide checks and balances to developers?

Awareness of AI Usage and Transparency

Governance frameworks must promote public awareness and understanding of AI capabilities and limitations. This includes transparency about when individuals are interacting with AI, educating users about data use, and building digital literacy. Awareness also empowers consumers and employees to make informed choices and identify misuse or manipulation. It also must include the potential for AI to become aware. While the mechanisms to do so become very technical, understanding at a high level how AI can become aware and its sources of learning will be important at high-level governance. Questions to ask:

- Are our customers, employees, and stakeholders aware when they are interacting with AI?
- Have we implemented transparency measures (e.g., disclosures, AI labels, consent mechanisms)?
- Are we promoting AI literacy and ethical training throughout the organization?
- How is the AI we use learning about us? When could it become self-aware?
- What would that mean?

Augmented Workforce Management

AI is increasingly used to enhance, monitor, or replace human labor. Governance must ensure ethical deployment of AI in the workplace, including fair evaluation, algorithmic transparency in performance management, and safeguards against over-surveillance or job displacement. Human dignity, agency, and skill development must remain central to workforce augmentation strategies. Questions to ask:

- Are AI tools being used ethically in employee evaluation, hiring, or productivity monitoring?
- How are we protecting employee rights and dignity in augmented or automated workflows?
- What training programs will be needed? How can it be designed to be agile and dynamic, since AI advancements are made weekly?
- What reskilling or upskilling programs are in place to prepare the workforce for AI integration?
- Who receives that training?
- How does this become part of the chief human resources role?

Unintended Consequences

Even well-intentioned AI systems can have harmful, unforeseen impacts, such as reinforcing stereotypes, displacing jobs, or enabling market manipulation. There are countless examples of early-phase autonomous planes and automobiles failing. For example, the Boeing jet crashes or accidents involving Tesla and Uber self-driving cars were the result of a combination of failed sensors, inaccurate data inputs, or a human being unable to take over fast enough. How can humans override a machine mistake? Governance must adopt a precautionary, anticipatory approach, requiring scenario analysis, stress testing, and impact assessments before deployment. Continuous monitoring and feedback loops are also essential to mitigate emergent risks. We already see the examples. An autonomous car loses the satellite signal, stops, and locks the passenger in the car. A self-driving car with a human driver has a malfunctioning sensor or is impacted by the weather, and the driver fails to react quickly enough. Automated human resource hiring tools limit the ability to consider qualified candidates due to built-in, unintended bias. Those are just a few examples. A Google report has identified four critical areas of risk in this regard:

- **Intentional misuse**: A bad actor or adversary changes the system to cause harm.
- **Misalignment**: Unintended consequences due to misalignment of goals and execution.
- **Mistakes**: The world is complex and a sensor misread or failure to comprehend information can result in harm.
- **Cultural risk**: Dysfunctional dynamics across the organization with the wrong culture or incentives, misinformation can cause consequences not intended.

Questions to ask:

- Have we conducted an impact assessment of AI systems prior to deployment?
- How are we monitoring for unexpected or harmful effects after deployment?
- Do we have an incident response plan for AI-related failures or harm?

AI Bias

Bias can be introduced at multiple points in the AI lifecycle, from data collection to model training to deployment. Governance must require robust auditing, diverse datasets, and fair evaluations to detect and reduce discriminatory outcomes. Questions to ask:

- Have our AI systems been audited for bias and discrimination?
- Are diverse datasets and perspectives used during development?
- What governance processes ensure fairness in outcomes, especially in regulated or high-impact areas?
- What are the sources of training data for AI programs? Are they defensible and credible?
- Have we considered how these algorithms are being programmed? Are there checks and balances in place to ensure "group think" is not plaguing its development? For example, if a bias is shared by everyone in development, it may not be corrected at the time.
- Are checks and verification built into the processe?.

Human Oversight

AI systems should not operate in a vacuum. Governance must require that human oversight is built into system design, ensuring that critical decisions are supervised, reviewed, or approved by accountable human actors. This is especially important in life-impacting domains like healthcare diagnostics, law enforcement, and automated decision-making in public services. Questions to ask:

- Where are humans involved in reviewing, approving, or overruling AI decisions?
- Do we have clear lines of accountability for AI decisions within the organization?
- Are oversight responsibilities reflected in job roles, policies, and performance metrics?

Human Override

In high-stakes applications, it must always be possible for a human to override AI decisions or shut down systems. "Human-in-the-loop" and "human-on-the-loop" mechanisms provide a necessary failsafe. Governance standards should mandate clearly defined override protocols to prevent runaway behaviors or erroneous outputs from going unchecked. Questions to ask:

- Can AI systems be paused, overridden, or shut down in real time?
- Are override protocols clearly defined, communicated, and tested?
- Who has authority to override or disable AI systems in case of malfunction or misuse?
- Are the potential unintended consequences mapped out to ensure that emergency human override is not only immediately available, but those who need to use it are trained properly on the system?
    - For example, when a series of Boeing jets crashed, the investigation uncovered that the Boeing pilots had not been trained to override the technology.

Governance Standards

A coherent AI governance framework requires consistent, adaptable standards. These should address risk classification, ethical principles, transparency, accountability, and compliance requirements. International harmonization is key, particularly given the global nature of AI development. Frameworks such as the Organisation for Economic Co-operation and Development (OECD) AI Principles, ISO standards, the EU AI Act, and the NIST AI Risk Management Framework offer a starting point but require ongoing refinement as technology evolves. Additionally, companies integral to the deployment of AI such as Google and Microsoft along with academics are building detailed white papers, both technical and policy driven, to develop governance and frameworks for AI. More work is needed to integrate these polices with intellectual property strategies. Questions to ask:

- Are we aligned with recognized AI governance frameworks (e.g., EU AI Act, NIST AI Risk Management Framework, OECD)?
- How do we ensure compliance with evolving national and international AI regulations?
- Have we established internal policies, committees, or risk registers to oversee AI governance?
- Are we engaging with external advisors or auditors to assess our AI governance maturity?
- How do we integrate thinking about intellectual property strategy to our AI governance models so it is not an afterthought?
- Should we be a leader, a participant, or an observer?

Beyond Policies: Director Liability in the Age of AI

As of now, there are no publicly known legal cases holding a board of directors personally liable for a company's use or misuse of AI. However, there are cases involving company use of AI and directors and officers (D&O) being named in the suits. Most of them stem from allegations of "AI washing" or overstating the capabilities or benefits of AI features, which can mislead investors. The risk is emerging rapidly, and several warning signals suggest that director liability for AI governance failures is very real and increasingly likely, especially in regulated industries. Consider the core areas of liability for board members. D&O insurance should be reviewed for appropriate AI coverage, if your business relies heavily on AI for delivery of your product or service.

Duty of Care and Oversight (Caremark Doctrine - United States)
Directors have a legal duty to:

- Monitor for compliance failures
- Ensure there are reporting systems in place to alert them of risks

Boards could be liable if:

- They fail to oversee deployment of high-risk AI systems
- No policy framework or reporting mechanism exists
- They ignore red flags like algorithmic bias or data misuse

Example: A company uses AI to automate hiring, and it is later found the algorithm discriminates against protected classes. If directors never asked about oversight or legal review of the AI, they could be vulnerable to claims of breach of fiduciary duty.

Securities and Exchange Commission (SEC) Enforcement

- In 2023, SEC Chair Gary Gensler emphasized that public companies must disclose material risks related to AI.
- Misrepresenting AI capabilities or downplaying risks (e.g., "AI washing") could lead to fraud or disclosure violations.
- Utilizing AI without transparency in financial analysis or predictions.

Directors who approve or fail to question misleading AI claims in investor communications could be at risk for securities fraud liability.

Federal Trade Commission (FTC) and Consumer Protection Claims

- The FTC has signaled it will go after unfair or deceptive practices involving AI, especially where automated decisions affect consumers.
- Boards may face scrutiny if they failed to oversee AI deployments that result in unfair consumer outcomes.
- Transparency about when and how AI is used.

Cybersecurity and AI-Enabled Breaches

- If an AI system is exploited or makes decisions that expose the company to a data breach and the board failed to ask about cybersecurity or model risks, this could open the door to:
    - Derivative lawsuits
    - Regulatory action
    - Reputational damage

IP Liabilities

- If trade secrets are unintentionally exposed by an employee, for example, via an unprotected discussion using AI tools
- If use of AI infringes upon the use of others' IP
- If what is created is duplicated because it is not protected when input into AI
- Failure to protect significant investments because of AI usage

Signals of What's Coming

- Shareholder proposals are increasingly calling for AI risk disclosures, especially in financial services, healthcare, and tech.
- The EU AI Act (enforced by 2026) and proposed US legislation introduce board-level accountability for certain types of AI use.
- Companies with weak AI governance may be viewed as materially mismanaging risk, opening the board to challenge.

Why Intellectual Assets Matter in AI Governance

AI does not operate in a vacuum. It is powered by, trained on, and outputs content from intellectual assets, including:

- Proprietary datasets
- Trade secrets and internal documents
- Licensed or open-source content
- Software code
- AI-generated content with potential copyright or ownership implications

Boards that fail to understand how these assets are being used or misused within AI systems may be opening the door to legal exposure, reputational damage, and shareholder action.

The convergence of AI and IP will grow exponentially in the years ahead, becoming a critical component of governance responsibilities. To close this chapter, we have provided a few helpful checklists to consider for directors and key executives responsible for oversight of AI governance in the organization.

Checklist for Director Individual Use of AI

Confidentiality and Fiduciary Duty

- Do not use AI tools (e.g., ChatGPT, Otter.ai, Claude, Gemini, Notion AI, etc.) to record, transcribe, or summarize board or committee meetings.
- Do not input confidential or non-public company information into AI platforms without legal and IT approval.
- Avoid using AI to draft or analyze board materials unless using a company-approved secure platform.
- Treat any AI use as potentially discoverable in litigation or regulatory investigation.
- Ensure that company-attorney interactions that utilize AI remain protected under client-attorney privilege (see February 10 decision: SDNY Rules AI-Generated Documents Are Not Protected by Privilege).

Ethical and Legal Use

- Do not rely solely on AI to inform or generate decisions on votes or board matters.
- Avoid using AI to write communications representing the board or company unless vetted for accuracy and compliance.
- Do not input board deliberations, personal notes, or legal advice into generative AI tools.
- Verify all AI-generated information against trusted, up-to-date sources before using in a board context.

Appropriate Use for Learning and Preparation

- Use AI for general education on emerging issues (e.g., cybersecurity, AI regulation, market trends).
- Use AI to generate questions or discussion prompts but apply critical judgment and human oversight.
- Only use AI platforms that are company approved or known to comply with security and confidentiality requirements. Ensure AI data sharing provisions are turned off.

Policy Compliance and Transparency

- Follow all company and board policies related to AI usage, including approved platforms and data handling protocols.
- When unsure, consult the general counsel or corporate secretary before using AI for any board-related task.
- Disclose any personal use of AI related to board preparation if there is a potential confidentiality or compliance risk.

Leadership by Example

- Model responsible AI practices to set a standard for management and peers.
- Encourage appropriate use of AI across the organization, starting with personal discipline.
- Emphasize the importance of human judgment, discretion, and oversight in all uses of AI.

Is a Private Company Less Liable?

While public and private companies both face ethical, legal, and operational responsibilities in using AI, public companies are held to stricter requirements due to securities regulations, fiduciary duties, and public accountability. Here's a breakdown of the key differences in requirements.

Area	Public Companies	Private Companies
Governance	Board-level oversight, fiduciary duty	Internal governance, more flexible
Disclosure	SEC reporting obligations	Limited; may be investor/ customer driven
Liability Risk	High (shareholder suits, media)	Moderate (contractual, reputational)
Internal Controls	Expected, especially for financial risk	Optional but recommended
Strategic Use of AI	Public disclosures for market signaling	Quiet innovation, less external pressure

Beyond policy statements, boards of all sizes should consider how they structure this into their current committee structure. While some established Fortune 500 boards have long since expanded the audit committee to include risks such as cybersecurity, many are now forming a separate risk committee. High risk companies may even want a more nuanced approach with a cyber and AI risk committee focused on understanding and reporting on the risks while overseeing deployment of the policies that have been written.

Armed with an understanding of the risks and questions to be asking, board members can begin to tackle the challenges posed by AI. Just like cybersecurity risk assessments, unfortunately, you are never done. Continuous review, assessment, and learning are required.

The governance of artificial intelligence cannot be relegated to a single policy or a one-time board resolution. Just as earlier waves of technological disruption from the internet to social media to cybersecurity reshaped governance structures and demanded new oversight models, AI is now accelerating the pace and raising the stakes. Boards, executives, and legal teams must recognize that AI governance is not optional but foundational to safeguarding intellectual property, mitigating liability, and preserving trust. The challenge is ongoing, adaptive, and deeply interconnected with every facet of corporate strategy. Those who proactively establish robust oversight, integrate intellectual property considerations, and embed accountability into every layer of the organization will not only reduce risk but also position themselves as leaders in a future where AI is central to value creation and competitive advantage.

Key Takeaways

- AI accountability requires continuous oversight, not one-time policies.
- Boards hold ultimate accountability for ensuring AI risks are monitored, mitigated, and disclosed.
- Effective governance demands cross-functional teams with checks, balances, and third-party audits.
- Intellectual property is at the core of AI, and IP strategy must be embedded into governance frameworks.
- Historical shifts (internet, open source, cybersecurity, social media, data privacy) provide lessons for AI oversight.
- Risk management follows three core approaches: internal mitigation, insurance, or outsourcing with indemnification.
- Directors face emerging liability under fiduciary duty, securities, consumer protection, and cybersecurity laws.
- Governance structures may need to evolve beyond the audit committee to include dedicated technology or AI risk committees.
- Policy statements are only the foundation – organizations need detailed processes, checklists, and ethical frameworks.
- Continuous monitoring, adaptation, and human oversight remain essential as AI evolves and scales.

CHAPTER 5

Where Should AI Oversight Reside Within the Organization?

The Implementation Challenge

Everywhere you look, someone is writing about AI governance. The term itself is becoming diluted by overuse, yet the urgency behind it remains real. AI could easily draft a governance policy, but only humans can interpret, implement, and enforce it. The more critical question, therefore, is not *whether* oversight is needed, but *where* that oversight should reside and *what practical steps* organizations must take to make it effective.

Beyond general oversight by the board of directors, effective AI governance requires a cross-functional model embedded throughout the organization. Oversight cannot live in a silo; it must connect across departments and disciplines. Moreover, AI strategy must be tightly aligned with intellectual property (IP) management because what goes

J. C. Wolfe and N. E. Cronin, *Owning Intelligence*,
https://doi.org/10.1007/979-8-8688-2388-6_5

into an AI system often includes IP (whether owned internally or by third parties) and what comes *out* may represent valuable new IP assets for the organization.

While various oversight models are being tested, lessons from three decades of technology and compliance governance suggest a clear direction: oversight should be led by a chief AI officer, chief risk officer, or general counsel, depending on the company's structure, culture, and maturity. From there, an AI Oversight Committee or Council should be established to ensure representation from key areas, each with an equal voice:

- Legal
- Intellectual Property
- Compliance and Risk (Including Open-Source Compliance)
- Cybersecurity
- Technology and Data
- Product and Innovation
- Human Resources

Ultimately, the board and executive leadership remain accountable for ensuring that AI initiatives align with corporate strategy, ethical standards, and regulatory obligations. However, forming a dedicated AI Governance Board or Oversight Committee, supported by clear policies, reporting mechanisms, and accountability structures, will help organizations operationalize oversight and minimize exposure to risk.

As AI becomes embedded in core business processes, the general counsel is uniquely positioned to lead the development of AI and IP policy. At the intersection of data governance, privacy, regulatory compliance, and intellectual property rights, legal leadership plays a central role in ensuring responsible and defensible innovation.

The general counsel's oversight is critical to:

- Navigate the legal complexities of AI-generated content, model ownership, and infringement risk.
- Translate emerging regulatory and ethical standards into actionable operational guidance.
- Align AI adoption with the organization's defined risk tolerance and strategic objectives.
- Capture and protect the value created by AI through an integrated IP protection strategy (see Chapter 7).

By assuming this leadership role, the general counsel helps the organization innovate responsibly while maintaining legal integrity, competitive advantage, and board-level accountability. In doing so, legal transitions from a perceived cost center to a mission-critical driver of sustainable innovation and enterprise value.

As AI technologies become deeply intertwined with business operations, the legal and ethical implications of their use demand centralized oversight. The general counsel is the logical anchor for this function, able to interpret complex questions around data rights, privacy obligations, and regulatory compliance, while also navigating the evolving terrain of IP law as it relates to AI authorship, ownership, and protection of proprietary outputs.

Legal departments already possess a holistic view across the enterprise, serving as the repository for transactions, vendor relationships, contracts, and risk management. This enterprise-wide visibility, combined with a deep understanding of both risk and regulation, positions the general counsel to serve as a strategic integrator, bridging the technical deployment of AI with the ethical, legal, and governance frameworks that sustain trust in the organization.

Further, while Goldman Sachs estimated back in 2023 that approximately 44% of legal tasks could be automated by AI, taking a proactive leadership role allows the general counsel and IP leaders to ensure that human expertise remains central to high-value, judgment-driven work.

Building Stronger AI and IP Outcomes Through Cross-Functional Collaboration

A cross-functional team approach ensures that AI-driven innovation is evaluated not only through technical or legal lenses but also with attention to its strategic, operational, creative, and reputational implications. Effective oversight requires collaboration across disciplines, blending governance with innovation management.

IP leaders play a pivotal role in determining whether AI-generated outputs can be protected and, if so, under which intellectual property regime: patent, copyright, trade secret, or trademark. Their responsibilities extend to advising on inventorship, authorship, and enforceability, particularly when AI has played a material role in asset creation.

R&D and product development teams are on the front lines of innovation and must work closely with legal and IP functions to document human contributions in AI-assisted work, identify potentially protectable outputs, and maintain records necessary for future IP claims.

Meanwhile, the head of IT ensures that technical infrastructure is secure, sensitive data is not inadvertently shared with external AI systems, and all deployed tools comply with the organization's internal security and privacy standards.

The head of risk provides alignment with the company's enterprise risk appetite, balancing the pursuit of innovation with prudent risk mitigation and liability management.

Finally, marketing and creative leaders play a key role when AI-generated materials are used in branding, content, or public messaging. They ensure that usage complies with applicable IP and publicity rights while preserving the organization's brand integrity and authenticity.

Together, this cross-functional team establishes a holistic governance lens for AI and IP decisions, one that identifies valuable assets early, assesses and mitigates risk, and ensures that innovation contributes to long-term enterprise value.

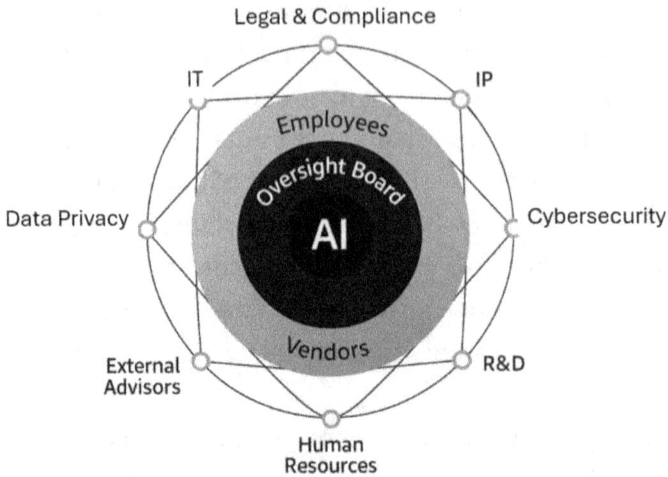

Practical Steps

Once the basic structure of AI oversight is established, leaders responsible for compliance and implementation should begin with a process mapping exercise, a structured approach to visualize how AI-related work actually happens across the organization in its current state. Process mapping, when tied to continuous improvement strategies, helps reveal inefficiencies, duplication, and points of vulnerability while creating a shared understanding of the current operational reality.

Six Sigma and similar well-established and proven methodologies provide a disciplined framework for this analysis. They allow teams to identify weaknesses, reduce variability, and design a path toward a more efficient and compliant future state. These approaches have long been used in rolling out IP development and open-source compliance programs, and they translate seamlessly into the emerging discipline of AI governance.

The process should begin by mapping the current state of AI usage, both at a macro level (organizational systems, policies, and tools) and a micro level (specific functions, teams, and workflows). It is essential that all stakeholders who directly or indirectly use or manage AI systems participate. Excluding individuals deeply involved in daily operations risks producing an inaccurate or incomplete view of the organization's true AI footprint. This exercise could be in the form of an audit, surveys, and/or interviews of key stakeholders and company business units.

Next, define the desired state, the target model of responsible AI use aligned with newly developed policies and risk parameters. Then, map the gap between current and desired states to identify the steps, controls, and resources needed to bridge it.

From there, leadership can develop detailed implementation plans, including timelines, milestones, metrics, and key performance indicators to monitor progress.

Admittedly, this work may seem like an obvious exercise, but it is not simple. AI oversight is a complex, evolving discipline, combining human judgment with automated systems that are still poorly understood.

Many large organizations have expressed frustration that traditional consulting firms are still experimenting in this area, often at the client's expense. Nevertheless, process mapping and gap analysis remain proven mechanisms for building structured oversight frameworks amid uncertainty.

The sooner the board authorizes a formal policy development plan, the sooner a cross-functional task force can be assembled to execute it, transforming oversight from an abstract concept into a disciplined, measurable practice. While large organizations certainly have more layers of departments and management, smaller companies can also apply these proven techniques to build out a process plan to integrate AI and IP strategy based upon where these functions occur in the organization.

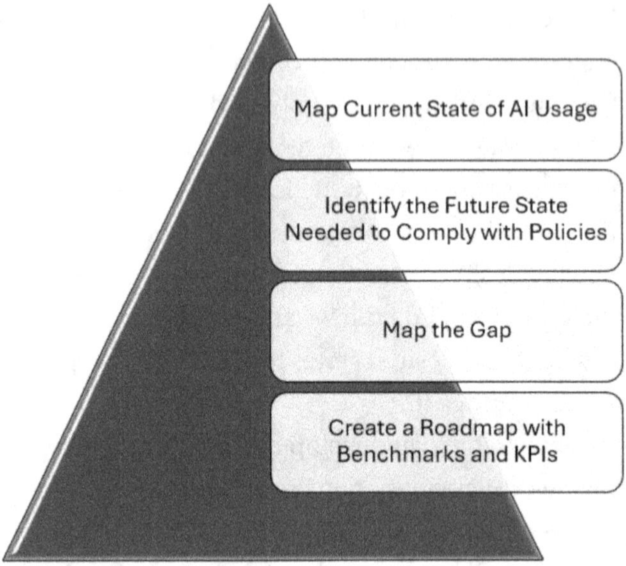

By applying Six Sigma and other process improvement techniques, organizations can create a strong foundation for developing AI policies that address all facets of usage, risk management, and IP asset creation. A comprehensive process mapping exercise brings structure and visibility to how AI is currently used, enabling leaders to identify risks, inefficiencies, and opportunities for innovation.

Across business units, a well-constructed AI process map provides a critical starting point. It reveals where AI is being integrated into workflows, who is responsible for its deployment and monitoring, and how outputs are generated and managed. This visibility helps the organization craft policies that are practical, enforceable, and aligned with enterprise goals, turning governance from a theoretical exercise into an operational roadmap.

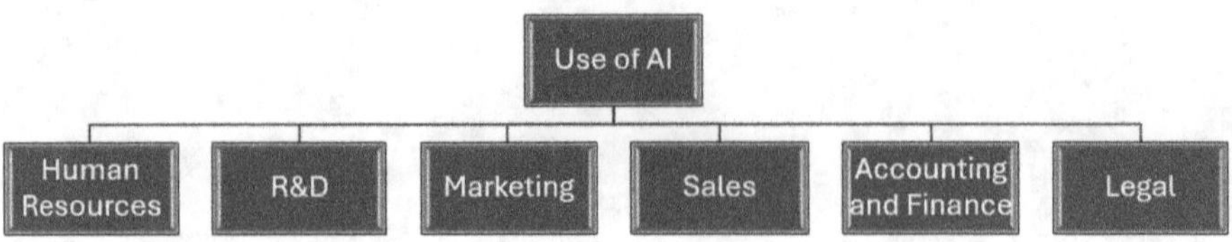

Once there is visibility into how each function uses AI and what outputs may require protection, leaders can begin designing the corresponding policies, procedures, and controls. The goal is to move from observation to structured governance, linking real-world use cases to clear accountability frameworks.

A disciplined approach involves continuously asking "how" and "why" questions across functions until a complete picture emerges of AI inputs, decision points, and outputs throughout the organization. This inquiry-driven mapping ensures that oversight is grounded in operational reality rather than assumptions.

Equally important is establishing checks and balances. Concentrating all oversight within a single function increases the risk that issues, biases, or unintended consequences may go unnoticed. Distributed governance, where legal, risk, technology, and business leaders each play defined roles, creates transparency, prevents blind spots, and strengthens the organization's overall AI accountability framework.

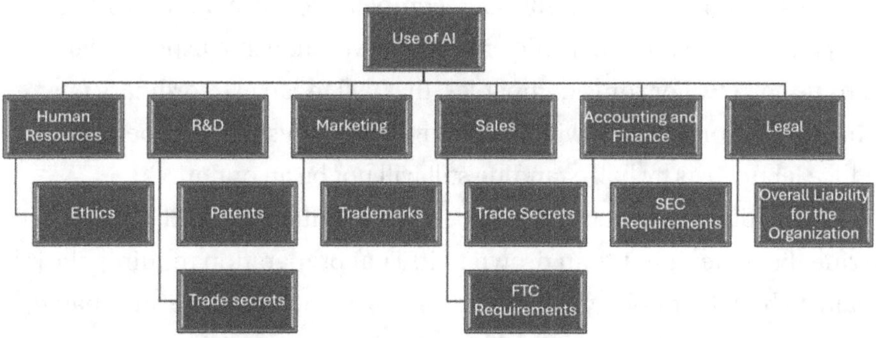

The Coming Tipping Point

Right now, the profitability of AI can seem like a mirage, highly publicized yet difficult to grasp in practice, particularly with the cost of using AI likely to increase. To many, the hype feels overstated, and the looming threat to jobs dampens enthusiasm for embracing the technology. In fact, to really effectively deploy AI and reap efficiency benefits that reduce costs and generate quality outcomes, a significant investment in human resources and thinking about integration with humans is needed. When budgets are tight, a band-aid solution offered by a software company or consulting company might seem like an easier fix, but without the actual thinking and hard work, the problems will later surface.

Further, the infrastructure build-out is massive, some of the tools are still clunky, usage by individuals and companies varies dramatically, and the returns seem uneven at best. But history tells us that technological revolutions rarely arrive as a gentle curve; they break open as tipping points. Once the systems are polished enough, once adoption crosses a critical threshold, the cost savings and productivity gains will seem undeniable. Every advancement in AI tools, which every day are becoming more "business friendly" to those unfamiliar with coding, brings the business world closer to the tipping point.

At that moment, executives will move from experimental pilots to wholesale integration. Businesses will rapidly adopt AI across administrative functions, customer service, logistics, compliance, and creative work. What feels like incremental efficiency today will snap into exponential gains tomorrow. For some companies, that will mean extraordinary new profitability. For others, it will be a survival mechanism. If competitors reduce labor costs by half, standing still will not be an option.

The leaders who prepare now, before that inflection, will be positioned to ride the wave rather than drown in it. That preparation requires clarity not just about technology, but about values: what should be automated, what must remain human, and what oversight mechanisms ensure accountability when machines drive the future of work.

The Human Talent Divide

As AI spreads, the workforce will stratify. On one side, there will be employees who collaborate with AI and team players who learn quickly, adapt, and bring creativity and judgment that machines cannot replicate. These individuals will rise in value, able to command better positions, compensation, and influence within their organizations. On the other side will be workers whose roles are easily automated or whose contributions fall into the "good enough" zone that AI can already match. For them, opportunities will shrink.

This divide will have far-reaching social consequences. Payroll tax bases may erode, threatening systems like Social Security. Communities dependent on mid-skill administrative and service work may hollow out. Entire industries may be reshaped, with fewer rungs on the career ladder for young professionals to climb. Unless education systems are restructured and new forms of social safety nets are built, the gap between the haves and have-nots could widen into a chasm.

There will, of course, remain jobs that AI cannot perform: caregiving, high-touch hospitality, and trades requiring dexterity and judgment in unpredictable environments. These will likely rise in value in the near term. Yet over time, robotics will chip away even at those bastions. The urgency is clear: workers, companies, and governments must reimagine training, reskilling, and incentives now, before the divide hardens into permanence. We explore the cultural and workforce implications further in Chapter 8.

A Roadmap for Boards and Leaders

This book has traced how AI reshapes intellectual property, governance, and organizational oversight. Now, at the threshold of profound transformation, boards and executive teams must act decisively. The roadmap ahead is not just technical; it is strategic, ethical, and societal.

1. **Define Ownership and IP Strategy**

   Companies must establish clear frameworks for who owns AI inputs, outputs, and models. Contracts, licensing, and governance rules should anticipate disputes before they arise. Treat custom AI models as core intellectual property assets, not just tools.

2. **Build Governance and Oversight Mechanisms**

   AI oversight must be cross-functional, with clear accountability at the board level. Establish AI risk committees, align policies with evolving regulations, and demand transparency from vendors and partners. The question is not if regulation will come, but when and boards should be prepared to demonstrate responsible stewardship.

3. **Prepare for Workforce Transformation**

   Develop plans for reskilling, redeploying, or supporting workers as AI reduces headcount in some areas. Invest in talent that complements AI, strategic thinkers, relationship builders, and innovators, while acknowledging that certain roles will disappear.

4. **Anticipate Social and Economic Ripple Effects**

   Companies that thrive in the long run will consider their broader ecosystem. Think beyond shareholder returns: how will your business model impact communities, customers, and employees? Will your adoption of AI deepen inequality or help to bridge it? These are not merely moral questions; they are reputational and strategic ones.

5. **Stay Adaptive**

   The trajectory of AI will be nonlinear, with sudden leaps and unexpected setbacks. Governance frameworks should be designed for adaptability. Periodic reviews, scenario planning, and stress-testing assumptions will be critical.

The successful leaders of tomorrow will be those who recognize that AI is not just a technology but a shift in the architecture of human enterprise. Ownership, governance, and foresight will separate those who harness intelligence from those who are overtaken by it.

Key Themes for Implementation

When studying the academic literature in organizational behavior and others trying to understand how AI will be implemented, a few key themes emerge for consideration:

Leadership matters: AI adoption succeeds when leaders communicate clearly, model inconsistent thinking (both/and vs. either/or), and emphasize augmentation.

Culture is essential: AI tools can either reinforce or clash with existing norms. Misalignment leads to resistance, workarounds, or shadow systems.

Employee perceptions drive readiness: Beliefs about AI's competence, fairness, and purpose shape whether organizations are actually "ready," beyond just technical capability.

Trust hinges on transparency: Workers accept AI feedback and outputs when the logic is clear, fair, and human validated. Opaque systems foster distrust.

Knowledge flows and collaboration shift: AI can accelerate knowledge sharing, but only under supportive leadership and learning-oriented culture. Otherwise, it reinforces silos.

Well-being risks are real: Anxiety, stress, and fairness concerns are pervasive. Addressing these is as much a human resources and organizational behavior task as a technical one.

Governance and politics matter: Red teaming and oversight aren't just technical; they depend on whether organizations create space for dissent, accountability, and independent review.

This cross-functional team can approach a few of the key action items per the chart below.

Cross-Functional Checklist: AI and IP Risk and Asset Evaluation

Action Item	Responsible Parties	Notes
1. Identify AI Tools in Use	IT, R&D, Legal	Inventory internal and third-party AI tools; assess license terms and data usage restrictions.
2. Assess Nature of Output	R&D, IP Counsel	Determine whether AI-assisted outputs are copyrightable, patentable, or confidential.
3. Confirm Human Authorship or Inventorship	R&D, IP Counsel	Document human input in all AI-driven processes to preserve IP eligibility.

(continued)

Action Item	Responsible Parties	Notes
4. Review Data Inputs and Training Sources	IT, Legal, Risk	Validate legality and source of training datasets (public domain, licensed, proprietary).
5. Classify Innovation Value (High/Medium/Low)	R&D, Legal, Risk	Triage IP assets to prioritize filings and protection based on business impact.
6. Conduct IP and Compliance Review	General Counsel, IP Lead	Check for infringement risks, open-source conflicts, or obligations under existing licenses.
7. Evaluate Risk Exposure	Head of Risk, Legal, IT	Assess potential liability if AI output is infringing, biased, or legally noncompliant.
8. Establish Internal Ownership Rights	General Counsel, HR	Ensure contracts, employment terms, and vendor agreements assign IP to the company.
9. Define IP Protection Strategy	IP Counsel, General Counsel	Decide on patent filings, copyright registrations, trade secret treatment, etc.
10. Align Brand & Public Messaging	Marketing, Legal	Confirm AI-generated branding/content complies with guidelines and doesn't mislead.
11. Maintain Documentation & Audit Trail	All Teams	Store documentation of creation process, AI tool use, reviews, and approvals.
12. Review & Update Governance Policies	Legal, Risk, IT	Periodically reassess policies in light of evolving laws, technologies, and business needs.

AI oversight cannot be consigned to a single department or treated as a compliance afterthought. It must be anchored in cross-functional collaboration, with legal leadership, particularly the general counsel playing a central role to translate evolving legal, regulatory, and intellectual property challenges into operational guidance. A governing oversight board or committee, reporting to the board of directors, provides the structure needed to balance innovation with accountability. Through process mapping, clear policies, and continuous monitoring, organizations can ensure that AI is deployed responsibly, transparently, and strategically. By establishing oversight at the intersection of law, risk, and innovation, companies can safeguard both their intellectual assets and their reputation while enabling AI to serve as a driver of sustainable competitive advantage.

Key Takeaways

Oversight Must Be Structured, Not Just Aspirational

- AI governance cannot be left as a vague "everyone's job." It requires clear lines of accountability.
- The board has ultimate responsibility, but a dedicated governance body (AI oversight board/committee or center of excellence) should manage implementation and report back.

Leadership Options

- Oversight may be housed with a chief AI officer, chief risk officer, or general counsel, depending on organizational maturity.
- Of these, the general counsel is uniquely positioned to lead given their ability to

- Navigate IP ownership, authorship, and infringement questions
- Translate evolving regulation into operational policies
- Balance innovation with corporate risk tolerance

Cross-Functional Collaboration Is Non-negotiable

- Effective AI oversight requires a cross-disciplinary team spanning legal, IP, compliance, cybersecurity, technology, product, HR, marketing, and risk.
- Each function has a stake: IT tracks tools and data, R&D documents human contributions, IP protects outputs, risk balances innovation with liability, and marketing ensures brand integrity.

Intellectual Property Is a Central Concern

- AI-generated outputs complicate inventorship, authorship, and enforceability.
- Organizations must triage innovation value (high/medium/low) to prioritize filings.
- Contracts, HR agreements, and vendor terms must clearly assign ownership of AI-driven IP to the company.

Practical Tools and Process Mapping

- A cross-functional checklist ensures consistent risk and asset evaluation.

- Process mapping (using Six Sigma or similar methods) helps identify the current state of AI usage, define the desired state, and close gaps with actionable roadmaps.
- Policies should cover acceptable use, transparency, explainability, vendor obligations, and escalation protocols.

Organizational Behavior Themes

- Leadership matters: success hinges on clarity, paradoxical thinking, and emphasis on augmentation.
- Culture is sticky: AI must align with organizational norms or risk resistance.
- Employee trust depends on transparency: opaque AI systems foster distrust.
- Well-being risks are real: fairness, stress, and anxiety must be actively managed.
- Governance and politics shape outcomes: accountability requires space for dissent and independent review.

Strategic Implications: Tipping Point and Talent Divide

- AI adoption is approaching a tipping point where incremental efficiency will transform into exponential productivity and profitability.
- This will widen the human talent divide between adaptable, AI-augmented workers and those whose roles are easily automated.
- Companies must prepare for workforce transformation, reskilling, and the social ripple effects of job displacement.

Examples from Other Companies

Based upon publicly available information, multiple public companies already have some form of AI governance function in place. AI assisted research produced the table below and may provide some guidance or input to what is the most appropriate for your company.

Company	Industry Sector	Where AI Oversight Sits	AI Policy/ Public Framework	Notes/ Comments
Microsoft	Technology	Standalone Office of Responsible AI (ORA); cross-functional Responsible AI Council; Board-level committee oversight	Responsible AI Standard; annual Responsible AI Transparency Report	Mature governance model; clear top-down structure (board ➤ executive council ➤ ORA); considered one of the most formalized AI governance models among public tech companies

(*continued*)

Company	Industry Sector	Where AI Oversight Sits	AI Policy/ Public Framework	Notes/ Comments
IBM	Technology	Responsible Technology Board (enterprise governance) + Office of Privacy & Responsible Technology (OPRT)	Responsible AI principles; Trust & Transparency commitments	AI governance closely integrated with privacy and responsible tech functions rather than a purely standalone AI office
Salesforce	Technology/ Enterprise Software	Office of Ethical & Humane Use (dedicated function); AI Trust Council (cross-functional); Ethical Use Advisory Council	Responsible AI Guidelines; AI Acceptable Use Policy (AUP); Trusted AI materials	Clear hybrid model: standalone ethics office + structured cross-functional oversight; explicit AI-specific AUP
SAP	Technology/ Enterprise Software	AI Ethics Office; Global AI Ethics Steering Committee; external advisory panel	Global AI Ethics Policy	Centralized AI Ethics Office with steering and advisory structures; policy explicitly branded as global AI ethics policy

(*continued*)

Company	Industry Sector	Where AI Oversight Sits	AI Policy/ Public Framework	Notes/ Comments
Google (Alphabet)	Technology	AI review function (RESIN) reportedly under Office of Compliance & Integrity/Global Affairs, later linked to Trust & Safety; separate Responsible AI research teams	Google AI Principles	Governance functions distributed across compliance and research; not structured as one single centralized AI office
Novartis	Pharmaceuticals (Medical)	Under Ethics, Risk & Compliance ➤ Compliance; AI Risk & Compliance Management Framework	AI Ethical Principles; Ethical Use of Data & Technology Policy; AI Handbook	AI oversight clearly embedded in compliance/ legal structure rather than tech/R&D; strong risk-based governance framing

(continued)

Company	Industry Sector	Where AI Oversight Sits	AI Policy/ Public Framework	Notes/ Comments
Unilever	Consumer Products	Cross-functional AI assurance process; leadership involvement from Chief Data Officer and Chief Privacy Officer (data + privacy governance positioning)	Responsible AI Principles; Responsible AI Framework	AI oversight integrated with data governance and privacy; not positioned as a standalone AI office
HSBC	Financial Services	AI Review Committee chaired by General Counsel (Digital Business Services); Group-level risk & technology oversight; AI Centre of Excellence	Principles for the Ethical Use of Data and AI	Governance strongly legal and risk driven; centralized review committee model with CoE support

(continued)

Company	Industry Sector	Where AI Oversight Sits	AI Policy/ Public Framework	Notes/ Comments
Siemens	Industrials	Cross-functional Generative AI Governance task force (technology, IT, cybersecurity, legal & compliance)	Responsible AI Principles; Generative AI Guardrails	Multi-department governance task force; operational guardrails for workforce use of generative AI

CHAPTER 6

AI As a Tool in Managing IP

In the previous chapters, we have covered topics including ownership of AI-generated works and governance issues. Let's now address some of the tactical issues in the use of AI specifically to manage IP in your organization. AI is rapidly becoming a component of any business that uses computation, digitalization, databases, and manipulation of data. Any processes that involve repeated tasks; heavy investment of time into data gathering, organization, and analysis; and regular reporting are clear candidates for the application of AI.

And this is simply where the journey starts. Simpler AI tools like robotic process automation (e.g., macros in spreadsheets) have quickly evolved to more sophisticated forms of code modules written (e.g. in Python), where more complicated instructions can be executed, and further can involve searching the internet, combining search results with company data, and presenting options, suggested recommendations, and conclusions. Now there are multiple platforms available for users to ask for code to be written without understanding a single programming language. The rapid advance of AI agents and agentic AI allows entire workflows with complex decision trees to be codified using GenAI. We are seeing changes in the AI tool support landscape daily.

J. C. Wolfe and N. E. Cronin, *Owning Intelligence*,
https://doi.org/10.1007/979-8-8688-2388-6_6

The history of AI was described in Chapter 2, but here is a recap of the terms that describe the spectrum of AI technology that can be applied in a given situation.

- **RPA (Robotic Process Automation):** Software that automates repetitive, rule-based digital tasks without learning or adapting.
- **Machine Learning:** A subset of AI where systems learn from data to make predictions or decisions without being explicitly programmed.
- **Neural Network:** A computational model inspired by the human brain that processes information in layers to recognize patterns and relationships.
- **GPT (Generative Pre-trained Transformer):** A type of AI model that generates human-like text by predicting the next word based on context.
- **AI Agent:** A system that perceives its environment and takes actions to achieve specific goals.
- **Agentic AI:** An advanced AI that can autonomously plan, decide, and act in complex environments over time.
- **Artificial Superintelligence:** A hypothetical AI that surpasses human intelligence in all domains, including creativity, reasoning, and problem-solving.

IP development and management are no different than other data-intensive industries with respect to harnessing AI for breadth, efficiency, and time saving. There already exist areas where AI is being used in IP management, and the list of areas is growing. It is safe to say that between the time that this chapter has been written and when it goes to print, the space will have advanced even further, with new tools created and launched. Companies may create their own bespoke tools or hire others to create them, and the market will undoubtedly offer platforms, subscriptions, and support for new AI-based IP management tools. For example, Perplexity added a natural language query IP search component to their product in October 2025.

While the purpose of this book is not to describe lists of AI tools for IP processes, nor teach the use of them, it remains useful to understand where and how AI tools are likely to be used in IP development and management in a company.

With a basic understanding of how AI can or will be used in IP management, a company can make better decisions if aware of the potential risks that AI use poses in IP-related activities. Further, management can determine what is an acceptable or appropriate use of AI in the intellectual asset management (IAM) process. Beyond that, what sort of employees should take on the role of AI-related IP management? What skill sets will be needed? How will companies work with both inside and outside counsel in the future, with AI as part of the process?

To discuss examples of how AI can be used in the major areas of intellectual asset management (IAM), the framework below can be used. For each category, some key benefits and risks are listed. Then based on that, an outline is provided of what an ideal "AI knowledge worker" for IP might look like in your organization.

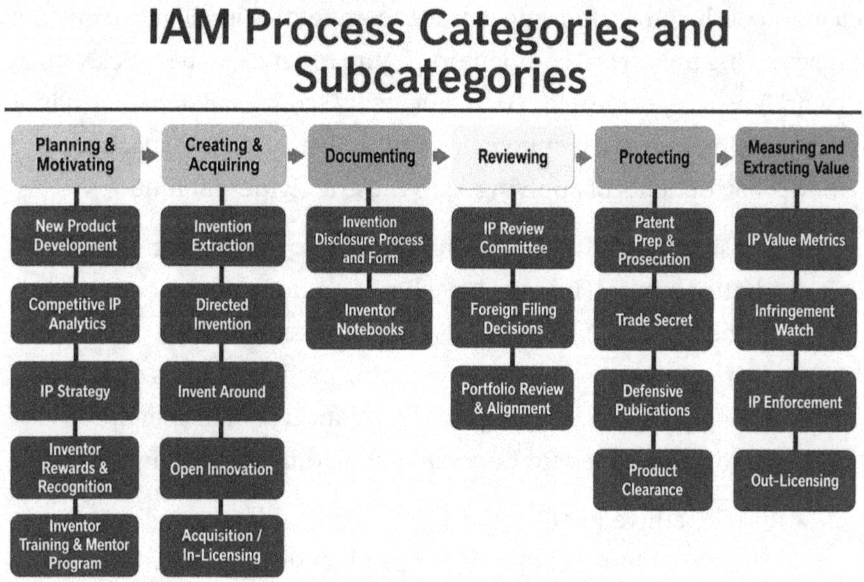

IAM can be defined as a set of processes to move ideas and innovations through a workflow to capture, protect, and gain value from them. In the figure above, there are many specific IAM activities that could benefit from the application of AI. Rather than speaking to each of them, we will present and discuss examples from each of the six high-level areas of planning and motivating, creating and acquiring, documenting, reviewing, protecting, and measuring and extracting value. For each area, benefits, risks, and suggestions are included.

Planning and Motivating

At the beginning of the IAM cycle, AI can be used to help inform the creative process. Generative AI tools such as ChatGPT/Codex from OpenAI, Copilot from Microsoft, Grok from xAI, and Claude from Anthropic (currently four of the leading platforms for GenAI) can help to do research on potential new products or services and help to identify competitors, trends, and craft strategies.

When seeking new product solutions and creating IP strategies to support development efforts, GenAI tools can be quite helpful to explore concepts, conduct research, and conduct competitive intelligence on known (or discovering unknown) competitors. Entire reports can be quickly built, and workflows can be developed to repeatedly scour available information for updates on products, technologies, and activities in your space.

Some key benefits of applying AI to these activities include

- Research can span larger bodies of information for better inputs. Humans have limits on how much time they can spend - and the level of sustained concentration - on searching information. AI tools do not get fatigued, can digest information at high speed, and can be used for hours on end without complaint.
- Competitive intelligence is no longer wildly expensive. It can be done at any stage of product development and repeated at any time for an update. No more limited budget for a single competitive intelligence study that becomes obsolete in a few months but can't be updated until next year's budget comes back. In fact, the search can be constructed to recur automatically.

- Fresh suggestions can be offered for areas of new products and services, outside of the typical thinking patterns of your team. Even if the ideas are not directly usable as is, they may prompt new thinking and novel directions.

The potential risks to your organization include

- Inadvertent (or intentional) use of material owned by others to inform research.
    - In a February 2025 complaint, OpenEvidence accused Pathway Medical of maliciously misappropriating proprietary AI prompts – essentially stealing OpenEvidence's intellectual property in order to use their trade secrets in their business. The case was filed in March 2025 so we will see how this case evolves and what precedent is set from it.
- Hallucinations or inaccuracies if information is not human-screened. GenAI is a large language model, not a keyword search tool. There have been improvements in fact-checking and GenAI models can be used to produce accurate output; however, dozens of instances of AI mistakes have led to embarrassment and liability for companies. For example, the *Chicago Sun-Times* published a summer reading list of books – and many of them were pure hallucinations that didn't exist.
- Over-reliance on AI tools could diminish strategic human judgment in IP planning. It is akin to teaching "first principles" – if you don't have a calculator, can you still multiply or take the square root of a number? Once there is a push button solution, if for any reason the AI is unavailable, will your team be able

to function without it? You may be "dumbing down" your intellectual capital without realizing it. From a Microsoft Research/Carnegie Mellon study, a survey of 319 knowledge workers led the researchers to conclude "*while GenAI can improve worker efficiency, it can inhibit critical engagement with work and can potentially lead to long-term overreliance on the tool and diminished skill for independent problem-solving.*"

Suggestions for your innovation and creative process:

- Draft company guidelines for how "fuzzy front end" product research using AI can be conducted in an acceptable way.
- Implement workflows that allow for human cross-checking of any AI-generated content. To avoid technical inaccuracies or ethical gaffes.
- Combine AI-searching with human thinking steps and assessment. There should be synergy between the two, so understanding of processes is not entirely lost.

Creating and Acquiring

In this IAM category, inventions are created or sourced, such as through brainstorming sessions for internal invention development, or via IP acquisition through partnerships, joint development, open innovation, or license/purchase of IP.

AI tools can be applied to inform and boost creativity sessions. Workflows can be designed to provide hypothetical situations, utilize brainstorming tools, and generate exercises for teams to create inventions.

Further, AI tools can also be developed to track collaborations, search for candidate IP, and conduct research on best matches of IP for potential acquisition. Tracking spreadsheets can be "smarter" and require reduced manual data entry and analysis.

Some key benefits of applying AI to these activities include:

- Automated mining of internal and external technical literature can suggest ongoing invention opportunities.
- AI support for time-intensive, repetitive activities allows for greater focus on strategic discussions and areas to add value to your products and services.
- Natural language processing (NLP) models help extract invention disclosures from R&D reports/emails.

The potential risks to your organization include:

- AI-generated inventions may raise inventorship and ownership ambiguity. Specific guidelines should be established to prevent full reliance on AI responses for creating and enabling inventions. Documentation of human inventorship, through content of expert-crafted prompts, can help in this regard.
- Risk of replicating or suggesting infringing concepts due to improper training data. Ensuring that AI results are fact-checked and freedom-to-operate assessments are made remains important when using AI for invention support.
- Legal enforceability of AI-influenced inventions may be uncertain in some jurisdictions. The USPTO originally issued guidance on AI-assisted inventions in March 2024 and then rescinded and updated that guidance in 2025. The topic is dynamic, so it's best to keep abreast of changes, but the current USPTO guidance is worth summarizing below:
    - Only natural persons can be inventors – AI systems cannot be named as inventors or joint inventors.

- The same inventorship standard applies to AI-assisted inventions as to all other inventions – there is no special AI rule.
- Inventorship hinges on "conception":
    - A definite and permanent idea of the complete and operative invention
    - A specific, settled solution – not merely a research goal
- The human inventor must possess knowledge of all claim limitations such that only ordinary skill is needed to reduce it to practice.

Suggestions:

- Instruct business units on where AI research can be used in invention development, for example, in brainstorming session preparation and options for technology components, systems, etc.
- Ensure inventors (scientists, engineers, product development teams) document their contributions to inventions vs. research conducted using AI. Teach them that currently, AI use alone does not constitute invention.
- Include fact-checking for invention research and enablement created using AI to avoid incorrect information.

Documenting and Reviewing

Off-the-shelf tools have been used for years to manage inventor notebooks, internal rosters of ideas, inventions, patent filings, and dockets. However, AI can be used to customize, update, and inform review committee processes so that companies can design tools to meet unique internal workflows.

Many companies may soon opt for a custom-built IAM workflow and supporting tools, in place of the expensive "one size does *not* fit all" software platforms, which tend to be inflexible in their use, content, and reporting.

Some key benefits of applying AI to these activities include:

- Natural language processing tools can help to draft invention disclosures and populate inventor notebooks. Handwritten notes can more quickly be converted to digital text, analyzed, and indexed across the company.
- The high variation of consistency and completeness of documentation can be evened out across teams. No more invention concepts on napkins, because AI can help significantly reduce the time and pain associated with invention disclosure documentation and submittal.
- AI tools can be created to triage and prioritize invention disclosures for IP committee review. The process for decision-making becomes faster and some recommendations can be nearly automated, with human oversight.
- Portfolio alignment tools can automatically cluster and map IP assets to business goals. This helps to visualize your IP portfolio and determine whether your filings are being aimed in the right direction.

The potential risks to your organization include:

- Erroneous or fabricated data ("hallucinations") from AI-generated text can undermine legal robustness. Human review is still critical for supportable invention.
    - At the time of publication, no patent or trade secret cases were available wherein hallucinations undermined enforceability, aside from AI-related incidents of legal procedure (e.g., hallucinated case citations). One such example is *Lexos Media IP v. `Overstock.com`*, where the plaintiff's counsel was sanctioned for submitting briefs containing non-existent cases and hallucinated quotations. In another example of a copyright case, *Concord Music Group Inc. v. Anthropic PBC*, Anthropic's legal team admitted that an expert's declaration included a fabricated citation generated by Claude. The court struck that portion of the testimony (`reuters.com`). A few more examples of AI-related legal mishaps are presented at the end of this chapter.
- Use of AI can result in vague or inoperable examples, weakening a patent filing. Human review of patent applications is still an important component of the invention documentation process. It is risky to use AI to generate patent applications and simply submit them as is.

- Sensitive IP documentation may be vulnerable if processed through unsecured AI systems. If a company uses AI tools, proper security and safeguarding of proprietary information need to be established.
- AI decisions may lack transparency, impeding justification to stakeholders or auditors. Thoughtful drafting of prompts and queries to help document rationale and decisions will help memorialize the decision-making process.

Suggestions:

- Assess invention review board processes to identify where AI can be helpful to add efficiency, such as creating a custom workflow to allow more rapid review of invention ideas submitted by employees.
- Allow employees to use AI to reduce time spent on documentation, such as voice-driven invention records, but ensure results are reviewed for accuracy.
- Evaluate whether AI-created tools to provide reporting and progress on invention KPIs can be used to improve internal (or external) communication regarding invention progress.

Protecting

There already exist various forms of AI-assisted documentation for patent applications, and these solutions will only continue to improve. Law firms and operating companies alike are assessing available tools for creating patent applications. Automated product clearance and prior art searches are becoming more common to support patent application development. Trade secrets can be more easily inventoried and managed, and trade secret management programs can be implemented using AI tools.

Key benefits:

- Speed in documentation will result in earlier filing dates and protection.
- AI can assist in claim drafting, prior art searching, and jurisdiction-specific filing strategies.
- Identifies optimal timing and cost-effective prosecution routes.
- Detects potentially overlapping third-party IP for defensive publication or clearance actions.

Risks:

- Errors in any form of automation used in patent construction could compromise patent scope or validity.
- AI-driven filings without human oversight may fail to meet legal standards, if not properly reviewed.
- If used for trade secret management, AI tool interactions could inadvertently expose confidential details.

Suggestions:

- Assess the company's appetite for the risk of automation. How much of patent drafting do you want to be AI-driven? What will be done in-house vs. what outside counsel executes?
    - Using AI tools may shift the balance of work between your company and outside counsel. It may be possible to bring some functions back into the company instead of needing outside assistance.

- Pay attention to mechanisms that help ensure humans are still inventors, as currently AI cannot be an inventor. Human review and revision of any AI-generated patent documentation, plus careful tracking of how inventions are created, will help defend your patent application.
- Design any documentation workflows for trade secrets to avoid sharing sensitive information to public AI systems that don't safeguard your inputs.

Measuring and Extracting Value

Assessment, metrics, and reporting are all areas where AI tools are highly useful. In the foreseeable future, models for IP valuation, monetization, and automation of IP lifecycle management will certainly exist and likely are being developed already. Tools for detecting infringement and competitor encroachment can be created.

Key benefits:

- AI can benchmark IP assets against competitors and generate real-time valuation metrics.
- Instead of costly and time-consuming research, AI driven systems can look for potential infringers or licensing targets via ongoing monitoring of patents, products, and literature.
- Licensing negotiations become less burdensome by using AI to model deal terms, negotiation scenarios, and varied royalty arrangements.

Risks:

- Incorrect or inflated AI valuations may provide misleading information for business or merger & acquisition (M&A) decisions, if not fact-checked.

- Importance of initial design: an AI platform could miss key patents, competitors, or licensing prospects. Any AI tool requires careful design, transparency in how searches are executed, and review by humans to confirm results.
- Licensing recommendations from an AI platform may not account for non-monetary strategic considerations.

Suggestions:

- Assess where AI-supported workflows for IP process will provide the greatest benefit with the least risk.

  For example, using AI to track incoming invention disclosures by number, source, and stage of development can free up team members for more strategic tasks.
- Obtain input from knowledgeable team members when creating tools for functions like IP valuation.
  - Embed their suggestions into the systems that are developed and allow them to participate in the design for best balance of AI and human functions.
- Include fact-checking of any AI tools that obtain information from third-party sources to ensure accuracy of results.

Key Competencies for Success in AI-IP Integration

What will be the right skill set for an employee to have to support integrating appropriate AI-supported IP workflows into an organization? Here are six areas you should consider for an ideal AI knowledge worker in IP. A single person may not have all these skills, but a combination of people can meet these objectives together.

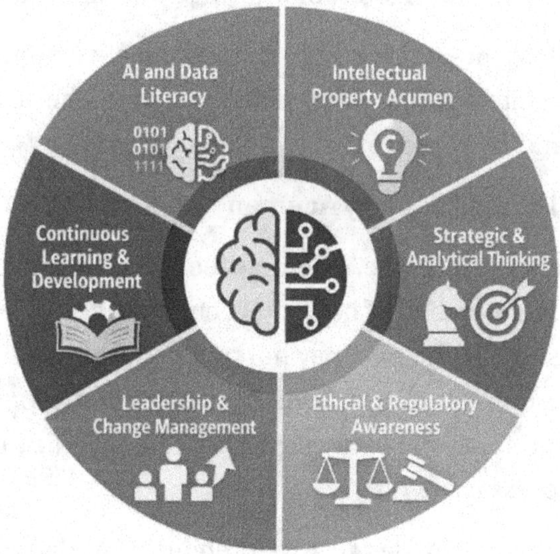

1. **AI and Data Literacy**
   Soon these skills will become expected of all knowledge workers. Some will have a deeper understanding than others, but a fundamental understanding of AI and basic prompt engineering will minimally be expected.

- **AI fundamentals**: Understanding machine learning, natural language processing, and generative AI to effectively integrate these technologies into IAM processes. More advanced knowledge workers will create and manage code for IAM functions.
- **Data management**: Proficiency in handling large datasets, ensuring data quality, and utilizing data visualization tools for informed decision-making
- **Prompt engineering**: Crafting effective prompts to interact with AI models, enhancing the accuracy and relevance of AI-generated outputs

2. **Intellectual Property Acumen**

   To work in an IP role, an employee will clearly need an understanding of how intellectual property works. While the role may not require legal education, basic fundamentals of invention, types of IP, and how they are managed in the organization are necessary.

   - **IP law knowledge**: Comprehensive understanding of patent, trademark, and copyright laws to navigate the legal aspects of AI-generated assets
   - **Portfolio management**: Skills in assessing and optimizing IP portfolios, researching IP positions, identifying opportunities for monetization, and mitigating risks
   - **Prior art analysis**: Leveraging AI tools to conduct thorough prior art searches, ensuring the novelty and non-obviousness of innovations

3. **Strategic and Analytical Thinking**

   Having a strategy will immensely help guide development and implementation actions. Creating workflow designs that align with company objectives ensures that the results are consistent with management views.

   - **Innovation strategy**: Aligning AI capabilities with organizational goals to drive innovation and competitive advantage
   - **Risk assessment**: Evaluating potential risks associated with AI integration in IAM, including ethical, legal, and operational considerations
   - **Decision-making**: Utilizing AI-generated insights to inform strategic decisions while maintaining human oversight

4. **Ethical and Regulatory Awareness**

   Company policy and regulatory controls need to be implemented in all areas, including intellectual asset management processes.

   - **Ethical AI use**: Ensuring responsible deployment of AI technologies, addressing issues such as bias, transparency, and accountability
   - **Compliance management**: Staying abreast of evolving regulations related to AI and IP, ensuring organizational adherence to legal standards
   - **Data privacy**: Implementing robust data protection measures to safeguard sensitive IP information from being leaked outside the organization, and conversely avoiding the use of others' IP in company work

5. **Leadership and Change Management**
   AI integration will require internal champions to lead the changes required.
   - **Team leadership**: Guiding cross-functional teams through the adoption of AI tools, fostering a culture of innovation and continuous learning
   - **Stakeholder communication**: Effectively communicating the value and implications of AI integration to stakeholders at all levels, and where necessary, guiding on risk management and decisions to protect the company
   - **Change facilitation**: Managing organizational change associated with AI adoption, addressing resistance, and promoting adaptability while ensuring "guardrails" are in place to prevent damaging actions
6. **Continuous Learning and Development**
   The AI technology space is evolving at light speed. IP policies are changing, not as quickly, but new USPTO guidance should be tracked. Staying on top of the changing landscape is critical to maintain competitive advantage.
   - **Professional development**: Engaging in ongoing education to stay current with advancements in AI and IP management
   - **Certification programs**: Pursuing relevant certifications or educational programs, where available, to validate expertise in AI and IAM practices

- **Networking**: Participating in industry forums and communities to exchange knowledge and best practices, and keeping open communication with outside patent counsel who can also be supportive and instructive in AI-supported IP development

With a team that is knowledgeable on the use of AI and understands the philosophy of your company, the AI workflows for intellectual asset management can be highly efficient, operate with proper oversight, and deliver tremendous results. Without a trained team or intentional use of AI process design, your IP workflows risk becoming slow and outdated or potentially can use AI in reckless ways that can damage your company's reputation.

AI is rapidly becoming part of every phase of intellectual asset management, offering new ways to accelerate what previously required days or weeks of effort. Companies can now realize increased speed, scale, and analytical power across planning, creation, documentation, protection, and value extraction. Yet its effectiveness depends not on automation alone, but on thoughtful integration. AI is a powerful tool that can augment human creativity, judgment, and legal accountability, rather than replace it. Organizations that establish clear governance guidelines, safeguard their confidential information, maintain rigorous human oversight, and invest in developing AI-literate IP professionals will be best positioned to capture the benefits that AI offers. Those that adopt AI carelessly risk legal exposure, weakened IP rights, and reputational harm. The future of IP management will not belong to AI alone, but to companies that intentionally design balanced, responsible systems, where human expertise and AI are combined in a disciplined partnership.

Key Takeaways

1. AI is reshaping intellectual asset management (IAM) across the full lifecycle – from idea generation to value extraction.
2. **Planning and motivating**: AI enhances research, competitive intelligence, trend analysis, and strategic ideation, but requires guardrails to prevent over-reliance and misuse.
3. **Creating and acquiring**: AI can stimulate invention development, mine technical literature, and identify acquisition targets – yet human inventorship and ownership must remain clearly documented.
4. **Documenting**: AI improves invention disclosure drafting, workflow automation, and portfolio mapping, while human review remains essential to ensure accuracy and legal robustness.
5. **Reviewing**: AI can triage and prioritize submissions, support committee decisions, and align portfolios with strategy, but transparency and explainability are critical.
6. **Protecting**: AI accelerates patent drafting, prior art searching, prosecution strategy, and trade secret management – without replacing the need for human legal oversight.
7. **Measuring and extracting value**: AI strengthens valuation modeling, infringement monitoring, competitive benchmarking, and licensing analysis, provided outputs are validated.

8. AI tools increase speed, breadth, and efficiency but also introduce risks of hallucinations, bias, infringement exposure, and data security vulnerabilities.
9. Human oversight, fact-checking, and well-designed internal workflows are essential across all IAM functions.
10. Clear governance policies must define acceptable AI use in IP development and management.
11. Only natural persons can qualify as inventors; AI remains a tool under current legal standards.
12. Effective AI-IP integration requires cross-functional skills in AI literacy, IP fundamentals, strategy, ethics, leadership, and continuous learning.

Further Examples of Problems with AI-Generated Information

Butler Snow law firm incident: In a high-profile legal case concerning alleged systemic violence and corruption in Alabama's prison system, the law firm Butler Snow submitted court filings containing fictitious case citations produced by ChatGPT. US District Judge Anna Manasco is considering sanctions against the firm for submitting false legal documents (Alabama paid a law firm millions to defend its prisons. It used AI and turned in fake citations | Artificial intelligence (AI) | The Guardian).

K&L Gates and Ellis George sanctioned: Law firms K&L Gates and Ellis George were ordered to pay $31,100 in sanctions for submitting inaccurate citations in a case involving former Los Angeles District Attorney Jackie Lacey and State Farm. The errors stemmed from AI-generated content that was not properly verified (Sanctions imposed for 'collective debacle' involving AI hallucinations and 2 firms, including K&L Gates).

Anthropic's legal filing errors: San Francisco-based AI startup Anthropic submitted a court document containing multiple citation errors due to AI-generated references. The inaccuracies led to legal challenges and highlighted the risks of relying on AI for legal documentation (SF startup valued at$61.5B sees legal drama caused by own errant tech).

CHAPTER 7

Building the AI-IP Strategy in an Evolving Global Policy Landscape

Over the past 25 years, the world has witnessed a remarkable evolution of laws and policies designed to govern business in an increasingly digital and interconnected environment. Frameworks for intellectual property, data privacy, cybersecurity, and internet governance have emerged through multi-stakeholder collaboration in an ongoing effort to bring order and predictability to a fast-changing technological landscape.

Yet regional distinctions persist. The European Union has long favored comprehensive regulation of privacy, data protection, and technology, while the United States leans toward market-driven innovation and sector-specific oversight. The BRIC (Brazil, Russia, India, and China) nations often impose even tighter controls, shaped by national priorities and sovereignty concerns. These divergences are unlikely to fade in the AI era. For global companies, understanding how these regimes align or clash will be essential to building an effective AI and IP strategy.

J. C. Wolfe and N. E. Cronin, *Owning Intelligence*,
https://doi.org/10.1007/979-8-8688-2388-6_7

As artificial intelligence transforms industries and creative expression, the world confronts challenges reminiscent of those that accompanied the rise of the internet, open-source software, and social media. Each wave of technological change has forced a rethinking of governance, ethics, and accountability. AI is no different, but its implications for intellectual property raise especially complex questions about authorship, ownership, and control.

Momentum is building toward greater international coordination at the intersection of AI and IP. How this develops will shape corporate governance, policy implementation, and oversight mechanisms that define responsible innovation.

The Intersection of AI and IP

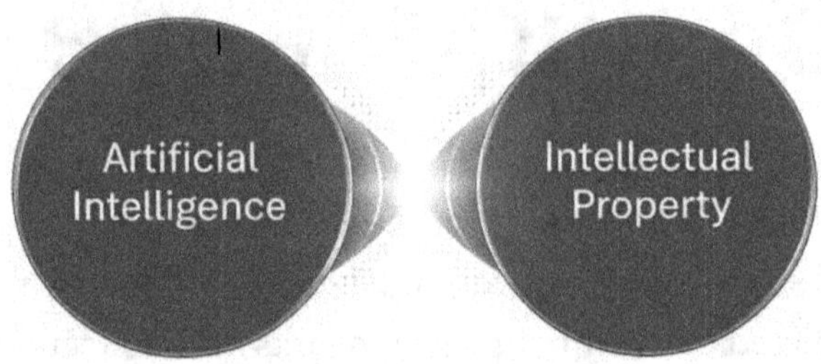

International bodies such as the World Intellectual Property Organization (WIPO) and the World Trade Organization (WTO) are well positioned to lead this coordination. They can play a central role by developing model frameworks for AI-generated works, clarifying ownership rights, and promoting interoperable data governance standards. They can also help build capacity in developing countries to ensure equitable participation in global AI innovation and enforcement systems.

Equally important, these organizations can serve as neutral conveners of multi-stakeholder dialogue, bringing together governments, industry, academia, and civil society to identify regional concerns, share best practices, and reduce regulatory fragmentation. By fostering collaboration rather than competition among jurisdictions, WIPO and the WTO can help bridge legal divides, minimize trade friction, and promote a fair, innovation-driven global AI-IP ecosystem.

Some initial guidance has been provided by WIPO via their 2024 document "Generative AI: Navigating Intellectual Property" and the World Trade Organization report, "Trading with Intelligence: How Artificial Intelligence (AI) Shapes and is Shaped by International Trade." Given the worldwide attention that AI has drawn, it is highly probable that groups like WIPO, WTO, and others will continue to examine the need for international AI policies and issue updates.

Ultimately, organizational leaders must decide whether to engage proactively in shaping these policies or to observe from the sidelines, remaining agile enough to respond once the regulatory landscape takes clearer form.

To govern cross-border AI innovations and disputes effectively, a combination of legal, technical, and institutional mechanisms is essential:

- **International frameworks and standards**: Develop consistent legal frameworks through international bodies that establish baseline rules on AI governance, data use, IP rights, and ethical standards. These should address liability, transparency, and interoperability across jurisdictions.

- **Dispute resolution mechanisms**: Create AI-specific dispute resolution forums, such as specialized arbitration panels or fast-track mediation services, under international organizations. These should be equipped to handle the technical complexity and multi-jurisdictional nature of AI disputes.

- **Mutual recognition agreements (MRAs)**: Encourage countries to recognize and enforce each other's AI-related IP rights, certifications, and regulatory decisions to reduce duplication and legal uncertainty.
- **Cross-border data governance**: Establish international protocols for data sharing, privacy, and sovereignty to ensure that AI systems trained or deployed across borders comply with differing regulatory regimes.
- **Transparency and auditability requirements**: Promote the adoption of interoperable standards for algorithmic transparency, explainability, and audit logs to support accountability and facilitate evidence in legal disputes.
- **Capacity building and inclusive participation**: Support developing countries in building legal and technical infrastructure to engage in AI innovation and dispute resolution on equal footing.

By combining legal coordination with practical enforcement and transparency mechanisms, the global community can foster trust and cooperation in the rapidly evolving domain of cross-border AI innovation.

Key Conceptual Points on Global IP and AI

Keep in mind the underlying tensions and constraints that drive different approaches:

- Traditional IP laws (copyright, patent, trademark) are built on the premise of a human actor (author, inventor, or using mark). Extending them to machines requires rethinking many assumptions.

- The more "autonomous" the AIs contribution (less human involvement), the harder it is to fit into existing legal principles.
- Some jurisdictions adopt or lean toward "hybrid" or "assistant" models: AI as a tool to assist humans, with protection tied to the human's creative or inventive contribution.
- Some proposals imply creating new regimes for AI-generated works/inventions (distinct from copyrights or patents). But so far, few jurisdictions have adopted such regimes in any robust form.
- Litigation (especially high-profile test cases) and legislative reform are still actively unfolding, so the landscape is in flux.

R&D and Patents in the Age of AI: Building the Future, One Innovation at a Time

What does this new wave of technological disruption mean for research and development and for the future of intellectual property? How are companies rethinking their innovation strategies, reallocating budgets, and protecting their creations in a world increasingly defined by artificial intelligence?

Despite AI's reach into nearly every sector of the economy, global patent data from 2024 and early 2025 shows that most filings still center on the core infrastructure of AI, its architecture, algorithms, and enabling technologies. This signals not only a race to apply AI but a deeper contest to *own its foundations*. It also means that future opportunities will emerge in the machine-human interface.

Core Areas of AI-Driven IP Development

Building upon patent data insights of Chapter 3, recent global trends highlight five key sectors driving patent activity and thus shape the future creativity and innovation landscape:

1. **Artificial Intelligence and Generative Models**

   AI continues to dominate patent filings, especially in generative technologies. As discussed in Chapter 3, companies such as Tencent, Baidu, IBM, and Microsoft are aggressively protecting innovations in large language models, image generators, and interactive AI agents. These patents represent a land grab for the platforms that will underpin future business models, creative industries, and knowledge economies, particularly in jurisdictions like the United States, where a *first-to-file* system rewards speed and foresight.

2. **Semiconductors and Digital Processing**

   The backbone of AI innovation remains hardware. Patent activity in semiconductor design, chip architecture (such as Nvidia), and high-speed data processing has accelerated dramatically. With AI workloads demanding vast computational capacity, companies are racing to develop processors that deliver higher performance with lower energy consumption, building the next generation of AI-optimized hardware.

3. **Clean and Sustainable Technologies**

   Alongside the digital transformation is a green revolution. Patent filings are increasing across battery storage, energy efficiency, and renewable integration, all increasingly augmented by AI. Intelligent automation now enables smart grids, predictive maintenance, and dynamic resource allocation, linking sustainability with advanced analytics in ways that redefine both cost efficiency and environmental impact.

4. **Biotechnology and Pharmaceuticals**

   AI is reshaping life sciences. Patent portfolios reflect breakthroughs in personalized medicine, gene editing (e.g., CRISPR), biomarker discovery, and AI-powered diagnostics. Machine learning is accelerating drug discovery timelines and enabling deeper molecular insights, transforming how diseases are understood, predicted, and treated.

5. **Cybersecurity and Data Protection**

   As AI adoption scales, so do the vulnerabilities. Patent activity around encryption, authentication, anomaly detection, and privacy-preserving technologies is surging. Organizations recognize that securing AI systems and the data that fuels them is not a compliance exercise; it is the foundation of trust and competitive resilience.

From Technical Arms Race to Human Integration

Amid this global competition, the next frontier of innovation is not confined to algorithms or hardware. It lies in the fusion of AI with human judgment, process, and delivery. The most transformative opportunities are emerging where machine intelligence amplifies human expertise: when a physician interprets an AI-driven diagnosis, when a predictive sales model informs a negotiation, or when a service robot enhances a luxury customer experience.

In this new paradigm, value creation stems not from what AI can achieve in isolation but from how seamlessly it integrates with people, physical environments, and processes. The intellectual property of the future may not be a discrete model or device, but a *system*, an adaptive ecosystem aligning data, technology, and human experience to deliver measurable outcomes. It may also expand into protection of trusted elements of brand design, colors, sounds and images.

Forward-looking organizations will direct their R&D toward embedding AI into systems of value creation, rethinking how work is performed, how services are delivered, and how intellectual capital is captured and scaled. Those who view AI not as a tool, but as an integrated partner in innovation, will define the next era of competitive advantage.

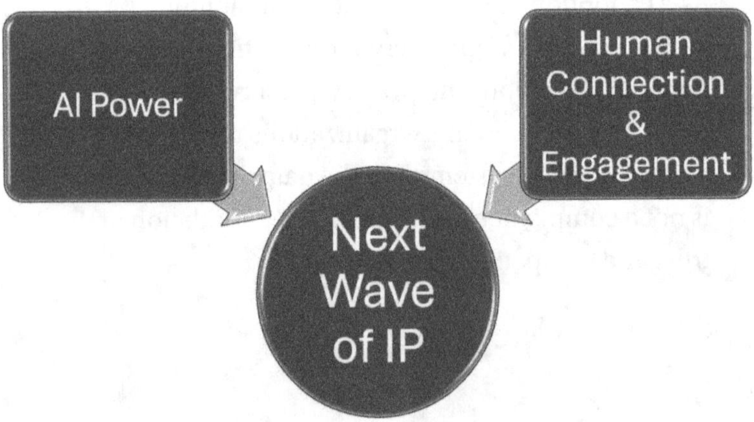

As we move into the next phase of the AI revolution, innovation will no longer live solely in laboratories or codebases. It will unfold at the point of contact where humans meet machines and where ideas meet execution. The *final mile* of innovation, much like the final mile of service delivery, will still belong to people. The difference now is that they will be augmented, not replaced.

To thrive in this new environment, organizations must design management, research, and delivery models that deliberately integrate human and machine collaboration. Mapping where automation ends and human judgment begins will become a strategic discipline. Identifying the points of critical human interaction will help leaders cultivate a workforce equipped not only with technical fluency but with emotional intelligence, the trust-building capacity that technology alone cannot replicate.

Much like the internet democratized access to information. Advanced coding capabilities are now accessible to nearly everyone. Management needs to understand that if decisions about innovation using AI are not considered and intentionally made, another company, or even an individual entrepreneur, may quickly outpace the solutions previously thought to be superior using these tools.

History offers perspective. At the dawn of ecommerce, many companies hesitated while Amazon recognized the powerful link between data and logistics. Two decades later, most retailers are still playing catch-up with Amazon's patented systems and processes. The lesson is clear: those who adapt early to structural change gain enduring advantage. The same is true now. Future leaders will distinguish themselves by how effectively they redesign processes to let machines perform what they do best, while empowering humans to lead where relationships, creativity, and empathy drive value.

New roles will emerge in human-machine orchestration, ethics oversight, design of adaptive workflows, and customer experience engineering. It will also accelerate demand for tools and environments that enhance, rather than replace, human capability.

Across the experience economy, from transportation to restaurants, hospitality, and wellness, the convergence of technology, AI, and human connection will become the new competitive frontier.

When it comes to reshaping organizations for this future, AI can help draft policies, handbooks, and procedures. But true transformation requires something no algorithm can deliver: process ownership, human buy-in, and shared belief in the mission.

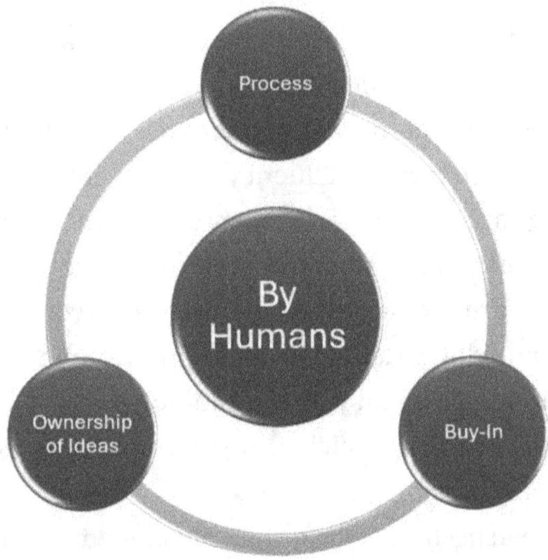

The best way to anticipate the future is to study the patterns of past transformations, how technology evolved, how quickly societies adapted, and what triggered acceleration. The pandemic taught us that adoption can advance at lightning speed when necessity demands it. In the AI era, new external forces - economic, social, or geopolitical - could again fast-track innovation and adoption. The coming wave of development will center on how humans interact and engage with intelligent systems. As that happens, we are likely to see a rise in design patents and non-traditional trademarks covering elements such as color, sound, and even digital personas that define and protect the next generation of creative and commercial identity.

From Foresight to Action: Allocating Resources for AI-Driven IP

Understanding where the future is heading is only the first step. The next challenge is operational, deciding how to invest in IP. As organizations translate vision into action, one of the most practical questions becomes: how should we allocate budgets to protect and create value in our AI-related intellectual property?

A well-defined AI strategy must include a corresponding IP and budget framework. Start by asking the foundational questions:

- How central is AI to our products, services, or operations?

  If AI is a key differentiator or core to competitive advantage, IP protection should command a proportionately higher share of the budget.

- Are we developing proprietary models, datasets, or tools?

  If so, resources must extend beyond R&D to include IP filings, trade secret infrastructure, and defensive measures such as freedom-to-operate analyses.

Tip Your IP budget should reflect your AI investment. The more your business relies on proprietary innovation, the more vital it becomes to secure and defend it.

Categorizing IP Needs and Costs

Breaking down AI-related IP activities into clear categories helps forecast spending and align investment with strategic priorities:

Category	Budget Items
Patents	Prior art searches, drafting, filing (domestic & international), office actions, maintenance
Copyrights	Registration for code, datasets, training materials, and model outputs
Trademarks	Protection for AI product names, visual identity, and licensing clarity
Trade Secrets	Legal audits, confidentiality policies, secure environments, employee training, trade secret registries, policies, and education programs
Defensive Strategy	Freedom-to-operate analyses, competitor monitoring, open-source license reviews
Enforcement & Monitoring	Litigation reserves, infringement detection tools, AI-enabled IP tracking

A company usually has a basic philosophy for how IP is used based on the specific nature of their business. For example, a company may highly value its barrier to entry (such as a patent moat) and seek to sustain clear freedom to operate for its products. Another company may instead seek to be the first mover, innovating and filing quickly and moving on as products evolve. Still a third company may seek to build a portfolio of IP for deal-making or licensing. Understanding where a company desires a high return on investment for IP, both for AI-related and non-AI-related innovations - can help to draft an IP strategy and lead budgetary decisions around IP investment.

Using a Strategic IP Matrix

To prioritize resources effectively, organizations can chart IP assets based on offensive and defensive value. What is important in this matrix is to identify the offensive and defensive value and then plot the business case for protection of either the technology or invention itself through patents, or design or brand elements through trademarks, design marks, or design patents, or if the asset is better served as a trade secret. These are established methods for planning IP prosecution and value aligned with business goals. Take a look at these charts.

- **Defensive value** reflects how well an asset protects your position, its legal strength, coverage, and exposure to risk.
- **Offensive value** measures its potential market leverage, how it can drive differentiation, licensing opportunities, or strategic partnerships.

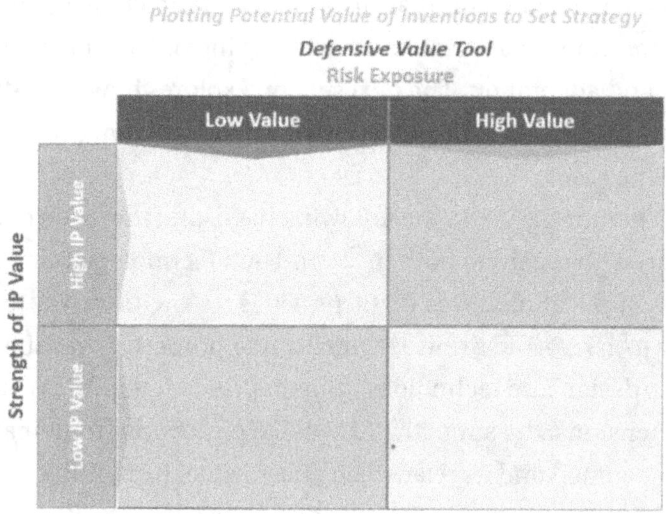

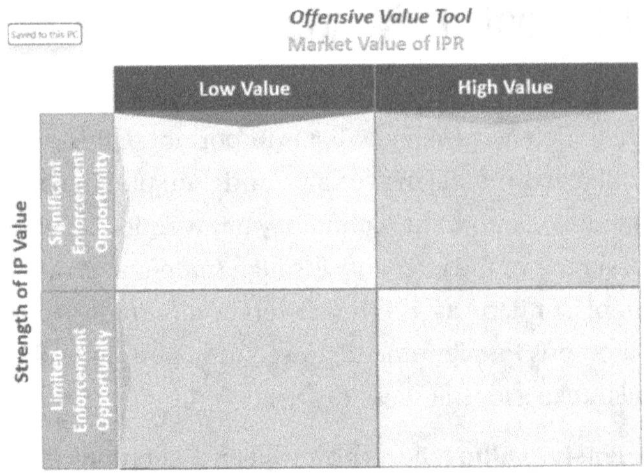

By plotting innovations on a value matrix, companies can visualize which assets warrant heavy protection and which should be monitored or deprioritized. This "IP triage" method ensures budgets are allocated where they yield the greatest strategic impact.

As budgets and policies take shape, leadership must also consider the governance mechanisms that sustain them. Protecting AI-related IP is not a one-time legal exercise, it's an ongoing process of oversight, education, and adaptation. The next section explores how cross-functional governance teams can ensure accountability and resilience in managing these evolving assets.

Finally, per the graph on the following page, plot the value of the asset on this chart with regard to both the brand and technology value and its business implications. This visual provides a structured way for an IP committee to assess and prioritize intellectual property investments across both brand/design and technology domains. Each initiative is evaluated on two dimensions: the strength of available protection (trademarks, designs, or patents) and its relative business value. By plotting assets on the matrix, the committee can quickly distinguish high-value IP that merits strong protection from lower-value elements where investment may be limited or deferred.

The framework then links the evaluation to action. For each category, the committee defines the appropriate protection strategy and clarifies the business implications, ensuring that IP decisions directly support product strategy, market positioning, and competitive advantage. Presented in this format, IP priorities become visible and reviewable by business leaders, helping align legal investment with enterprise objectives.

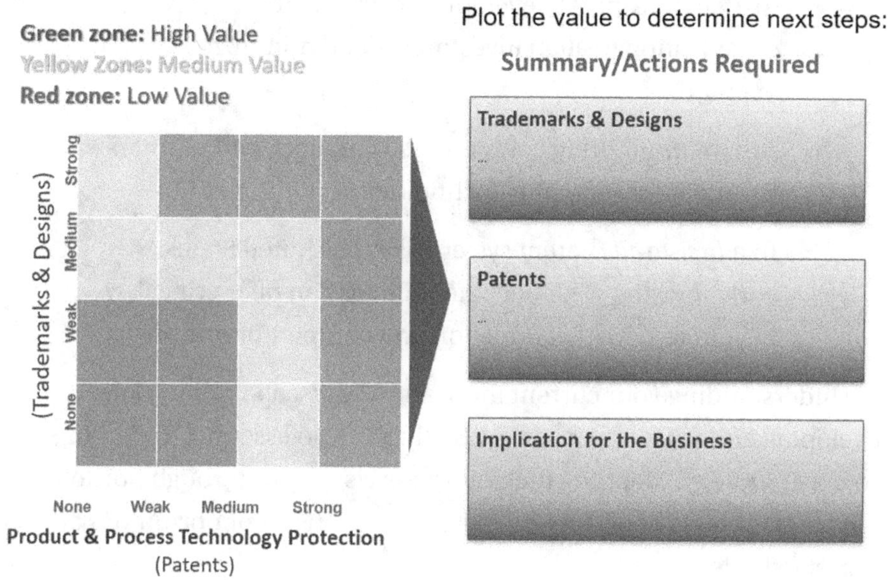

This framework provides a structured way to evaluate the investment value of protecting your AI-related assets within a cross-functional strategy and aligning it to the business strategy and implications.

Evaluating the Innovation Pipeline

Building a sustainable AI-IP strategy requires more than protecting what already exists; it demands visibility into what's coming next. Begin by assessing the strength, scale, and focus of your innovation pipeline.

Ask:

- How many AI-related innovations are we generating annually or contemplating developing in the foreseeable future?
- What is the projected commercial value of these assets?
- Are we tracking AI development across the organization to align investments and minimize overlap?
- Are we monitoring competitors, suppliers, and partners to anticipate emerging technologies?

  In a *first-to-file* patent system like the United States, early tracking of global patent filings can offer critical insight into market direction and competitor priorities.

Understanding your current innovation landscape, what you're developing and what others are protecting, is also essential to shaping a proactive strategy. Mapping these answers visually or through portfolio management tools helps reveal where your strongest opportunities and highest risks lie.

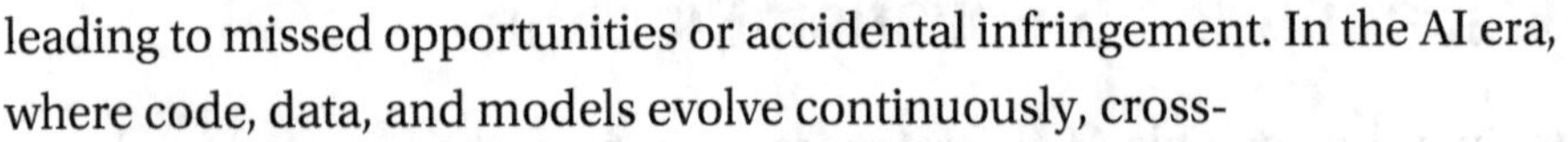

Equally important, integrate IP thinking throughout the development lifecycle, not just at the end. Too often, organizations treat IP as a final step, leading to missed opportunities or accidental infringement. In the AI era, where code, data, and models evolve continuously, cross-functional collaboration between legal, R&D, and business teams is key to minimizing risk and maximizing value.

AI tools themselves can assist in this analysis, scanning patent databases, clustering technology domains, and identifying overlaps, *but human judgment remains essential* to validate insights, interpret exposure, and ensure nothing critical is overlooked. More detail on the use of AI in IP activities was discussed in Chapter 6.

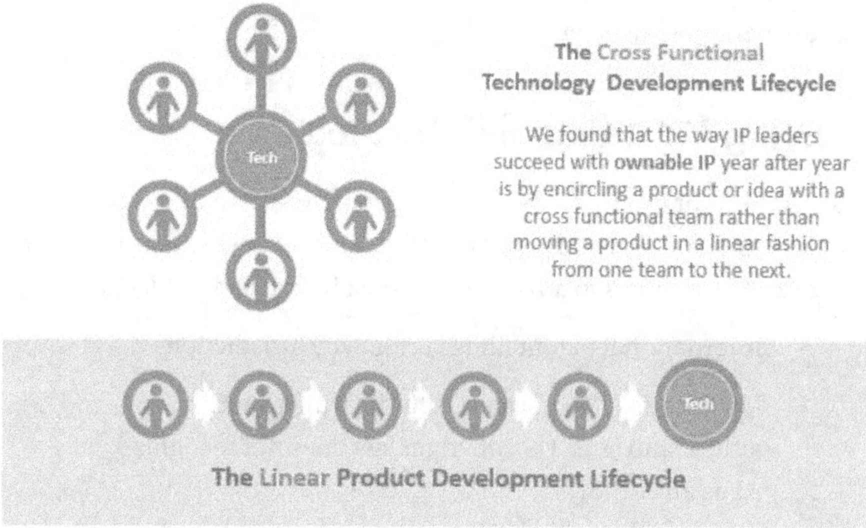

Embedding AI-Specific IP Governance

Budget and planning should include a clear governance layer dedicated to AI-related IP. This ensures consistency, compliance, and strategic foresight. Consider funding for:

- Legal and technical staff training on AI and IP fundamentals
- Regular IP audits for AI-generated outputs
- Frameworks to document authorship, ownership, and model provenance

- Enforcement of AI usage and disclosure policies
- Tools that detect AI-generated IP risks (e.g., code scanning, dataset lineage verification)

Ensure that AI is a persistent topic of discussion within IP governance functions, workflows, and checklists. It should become a standard element of assessment in IP oversight.

Planning for a Global IP Strategy

If your AI tools or products operate across borders, plan early for the complexity of global protection. The guidance and laws can be expected to change as AI continues to advance and must be tracked. Budget for:

- International patent filings under key jurisdictions
- Local counsel to navigate differing rules on AI authorship (e.g., US copyright law does not recognize AI as an author)
- Ongoing monitoring of AI regulations in major markets such as the EU, the UK, China, and India

A coordinated global filing and monitoring strategy not only reduces risk but also signals leadership and credibility in emerging markets.

Budgeting for Enforcement

Protection without enforcement has limited value. If your business model depends on exclusive AI technology, plan proactively for:

- Ongoing monitoring of infringement and scraping activity
- Budget reserves for litigation or arbitration

- IP insurance coverage to offset enforcement costs
- Potentially trade secret insurance if your data is highly proprietary. Private databases are highly valuable as a source for internal AI tools

Integrating these considerations into your annual planning process creates a living framework - one that evolves as fast as the technology itself.

Bringing It All Together: Prioritization, Governance, and Strategic Foresight

To allocate budgets and resources effectively, organizations must treat intellectual asset management as a living system, not a one-time exercise. Begin by triaging AI-related assets into high-, medium-, and low-value tiers based on strategic relevance, competitive advantage, and enforceability:

- **High-value assets** protect core AI algorithms, proprietary datasets, and innovations central to revenue generation or market differentiation. These demand comprehensive protection through patents, trade secrets, and robust enforcement mechanisms.
- **Medium-value assets** - such as product enhancements, applied models, or branding elements - warrant selective filings or internal safeguards but not full-scale global protection.
- **Low-value assets**, including routine outputs, generic tools, or experimental prototypes, may be documented and monitored with minimal budget until they mature into higher-value innovations. These can be protected simply through company policies of use.

This disciplined triage ensures that IP investment aligns with true business impact, optimizing both protection and profitability.

But strategy alone is not enough. Effective AI Governance requires more than traditional board oversight; it demands a cross-functional framework that embeds accountability, transparency, and continuous learning into the organization. Legal, R&D, compliance, cybersecurity, and operations teams must work in concert, providing checks and balances, sharing insights, and surfacing risks and opportunities in real time.

Ultimately, artificial intelligence and intellectual property is not merely a legal matter; it is a strategic battleground that will determine which companies thrive in the next era of global commerce. Just as the internet, ecommerce, and data privacy once redefined competitive advantage, the AI era will require organizations to anticipate policy shifts, harmonize compliance across borders, potentially change how internal teams operate, and embed IP strategy into every stage of innovation.

Those who understand this interplay, who align governance, investment, and human expertise with AI-driven capability, will secure not only legal protection, but sustained market leadership. The lesson from past disruptions remains clear: companies that wait to adapt will find themselves chasing the future, while those who act now will be the ones defining it.

The organizations that will lead in the AI era are those that treat intellectual property not as paperwork or as a function delegated solely to AI, but as part of their business strategy, using AI tempered with human judgment. By prioritizing high-value assets, embedding cross-functional governance, and aligning investment with business impact, leaders can transform IP from a cost center into a competitive weapon. The future of innovation belongs to those who see AI and IP as interdependent forces, one powering discovery, the other securing its value. In an age where intelligence itself can be created, owned, and scaled, the real differentiator will be foresight: the ability to act before the rules are written.

Key Takeaways

- **Global divergence matters**: Regulatory landscapes for AI and IP vary across regions, with the EU highly regulated, the United States more flexible, and the BRIC countries often restrictive.
- **Coordination is coming**: International organizations such as WIPO, WTO, and OECD are likely to lead harmonization efforts through frameworks, capacity-building, and dispute resolution.
- **Patent race is foundational**: Most current AI-related patents focus on infrastructure – algorithms, architecture, and chips – highlighting the urgency to secure core technologies.
- **Innovation spans industries**: Key areas of growth include generative AI, semiconductors, clean tech, biotech, and cybersecurity, each reshaping competitive dynamics.
- **Integration is the frontier**: The next wave of value lies in blending AI with human judgment and service delivery, especially in sectors where trust, relationships, and experience drive differentiation.
- **Budget alignment is critical**: AI-IP investment must track business strategy, distinguishing high-value assets that warrant robust protection from lower-value innovations that may only need limited safeguards.

- **Governance must be cross-functional**: Boards provide oversight, but cross-functional teams are essential to balance innovation, compliance, and risk management.
- **Adaptation wins**: Companies that integrate AI into their processes and workforce models with foresight will be better positioned to lead, much like how Amazon mastered ecommerce through logistics and data strategy.

CHAPTER 8

The Silent Disruption: How AI Is Rewriting the Rules of Work and Organizational Behavior

From the perspective of a futurist, how will AI change work behavior and influence new areas of innovation in the next decade? When and how will this ultimately converge with the question of ownership over intelligence?

For years, AI leaders and futurists have been sounding the alarm: artificial intelligence will replace jobs. At first, these warnings were treated as speculative or reserved for a distant future. But today, the future is arriving faster than many anticipated. With each passing day, AI tools become more capable, not only streamlining repetitive tasks but fundamentally reshaping how we work, think, and organize.

J. C. Wolfe and N. E. Cronin, *Owning Intelligence*,
https://doi.org/10.1007/979-8-8688-2388-6_8

The early impact zones are predictable: administrative roles, research assistants, and analytical support positions are already under pressure. As AI becomes adept at drafting emails, summarizing research, and generating content, knowledge work is undergoing a quiet revolution. These are not jobs of the past; they are today's white-collar professions. Yet rather than eliminating all human roles, AI is sharpening the divide between those who merely consume information and those who can synthesize, evaluate, and act on it with judgment and nuance.

Contrary to the dystopian fear that AI will make us dumber, the opposite is becoming true: AI will make *smart humans* stand out. When everyone has access to AI, the differentiator becomes not just how well you prompt a tool, but how well you *think*. In a world where AI is everywhere, human discernment, critical thinking, and domain expertise become premium skills. Eventually, those who over-rely on AI without understanding will be exposed when asked to think on their feet, speak without a script, or correct AI's occasionally wrong outputs.

So far, the disruption has primarily affected the professional class who largely work in an office using computers. But the convergence of AI with robotics and integration into business enterprise platforms promises to eventually extend the transformation to blue-collar and service jobs. As physical machines become smarter, faster, and more adaptable, the next wave of disruption will sweep through warehouses, kitchens, factories, and retail.

What's more, the ability to mask AI's involvement, whether in a proposal, a design, or a customer interaction will be short lived. Clients, regulators, and peers will demand transparency. Organizations that fail to adapt will find themselves not only outpaced but distrusted.

In this new world, leadership is no longer about controlling human workflows alone. It's about guiding the behavior of systems where AI is a co-worker, a tool, and a risk factor. Understanding how individuals, teams, and entire enterprises respond to the integration of AI is the next frontier of organizational strategy. Success will belong to those leaders who can manage not just people, but the interface between human talent and machine capability.

Throughout this book, we have woven the concept of intellectual property as a key input into AI tools and the ultimate output from it as well. Accordingly, understanding the basic tenets of how it will disrupt the workforce and what types of new organizational behavior may emerge is important to prepare the policies, processes, and standards that will be necessary to succeed.

Fundamentally, what will not change is the desire and need for human relationships with trusted advisors and team members. So as you consider the changes that will undoubtedly come with AI usage, also consider the core relationships that will be so fundamental to human living. A trusted accountant might use AI to rapidly increase the speed of tax preparation or number crunching, but it is the trust in that person to advise you, to help you make important decisions using that information, that will not simply transfer over to a machine or a computer. Likewise, a lawyer may use AI tools to analyze case law, prepare contracts or aggregate data, but their counsel and wisdom will remain the core value proposition.

We have, ourselves, carefully used AI in the process of researching, refining, editing, and creating this book. In our own experience, we have found that a carefully thought-out, well-worded prompt alone is never sufficient. A great editing partner, yes. But copy and paste, no. A great research assistant, yes, but do citations need to be checked, yes.

The Future of Work in the AI Era

Over the next two to seven years, the fusion of AI with business operations will catalyze a profound restructuring of labor, wealth, and opportunity, but some of this has already started.

Quiet Shifts Already Underway

In many large companies, workforce transformation is happening quietly, under the cover of routine HR policies:

- **Attrition without replacement**: Departing employees are not being replaced, leading to slow but steady reductions in headcount.
- **"Invisible" efficiencies:** AI is allowing teams to do more with the current headcount. This is a subtle difference from attrition. Companies are achieving production growth without headcount growth.
- **Early retirement incentives**: Firms are encouraging older employees, particularly in soon-to-be-automated roles, or management roles that may no longer be needed to leave early, with no intention of filling their jobs.
- **Reorganization of teams**: Cross-functional teams are being restructured to embed AI into daily workflows, while firms identify and cultivate workers who can thrive in an AI-enhanced environment.

These quiet contractions feel less disruptive than mass layoffs, but they are laying the groundwork for sharper, more painful changes.

The Coming Inflection Point

Once AI systems demonstrate undeniable productivity gains, workforce reductions will accelerate and become explicit.

The First Wave: Underperformers

AI-powered analytics will enable companies to precisely identify and shed low-performing workers, those with chronic underperformance, poor attendance, or low engagement. These workers will struggle to find employment, often relegated to manual labor roles until robotics eventually replaces those as well. This will also free up management time to focus on developing high performers instead of chasing down the poor performers.

The Second Wave: The Average Majority

The more destabilizing shift will strike the middle of the workforce. Average employees, once the backbone of the corporate world, will be displaced as high performers with AI tools can do the work of many.

This will create a new divide: those who adapt, reskill, and rise with AI and those left behind. Whether this is three to five years away as some suggest or 18–24 months as we believe, organizations need to be thinking now about how they prepare their structure and the workforce itself for these coming changes. Some have conservatively suggested these changes are decades away, but that seems unlikely for all but those jobs where performance is heavily human labor driven. Government leaders and policy influencers need to think about what shifts in tax policy and government support for education and skill building may be needed in a new era.

The need for mental health support, skill building in a new era, and human resource management will explode in the years ahead.

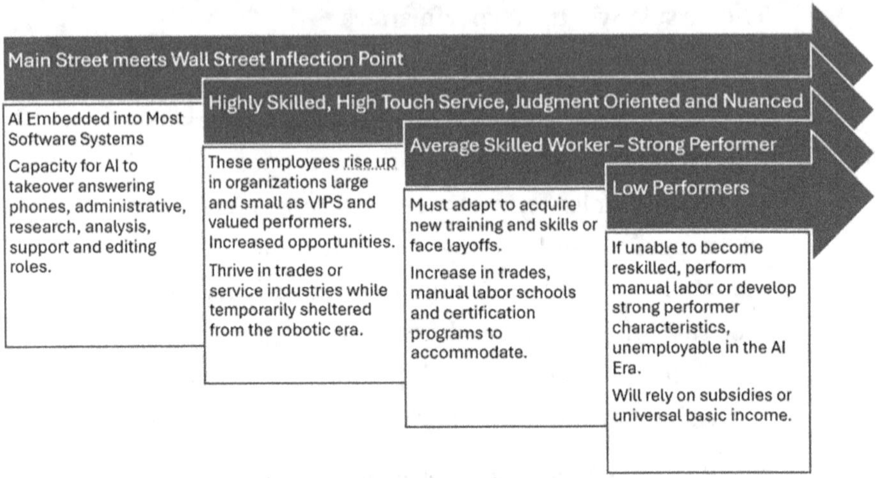

The integration of artificial intelligence into nearly all software systems will reshape the labor market in both large corporations and small businesses alike. And it will likely converge on Wall Street and Main Street in the next 12–24 months. As AI takes over many customer service, administrative, research, analysis, and support roles, the workforce will begin to divide based upon adaptability, judgment, and skill. In fact, the way that many businesses operate will change. Workers will increasingly become managers of AI functions, a cross-check and quality control mechanism that allows AI applications to be incorporated without loss of accuracy, ethics, or legality. This fundamentally changes workflows in commerce.

Highly skilled, high-touch employees, those with nuanced judgment and human-centric expertise, will rise in value. They become VIPs within organizations, thriving in roles that require intelligence, decision-making, and interpersonal connection. Many will find refuge and growth in trades and service industries that are less exposed, at least temporarily, to automation.

Average skilled workers who perform strongly must adapt by retraining or acquiring new technical and interpersonal skills to remain relevant. The growing demand for trade schools, manual labor training, and certification programs reflects this transition as workers reposition themselves in a rapidly changing market.

Low performers, however, face significant risk. Without reskilling or the ability to demonstrate consistent strong performance, they may find themselves unemployable in the AI era. Many in this group could come to depend on government subsidies or universal basic income.

This moment marks a profound inflection point where AI's efficiency collides with human adaptability, reshaping not just industries, but the very definition of value and work.

Artificial intelligence is not simply another wave of automation; it is a silent disruptor that is rewriting the rules of work, reshaping organizational behavior, and redrawing the boundary between human and machine contribution. Over the next decade, its influence will ripple across industries in ways as transformative as the internet, but with deeper reach into both cognitive and physical labor. The advantage will not belong to those who master prompts, but to those who cultivate judgment, expertise, and the trust that only human relationships can sustain.

Leaders must embrace AI as a co-worker, a collaborator, and, at times, a competitor while also preparing their organizations for the ethical, legal, and cultural shifts that will inevitably follow. What endures is not the task itself, but the uniquely human capacity to connect, advise, and create meaning. Those who blend AI's efficiency with human discernment will thrive in this new era of innovation.

Further, strong organizational leadership needs to be developing the training pipeline of the future. How will young people starting their careers develop the skills, judgment, and nuance needed? This will require rethinking the career path and human resource plan for most organizations.

We wrote more about our experience using AI in the opening and closing chapters, but as we use AI for what it's most valuable at, let's look at the industries AI believes will be transformed or disrupted (and many have already begun this transformation). Note that based upon carefully nuanced prompts, this is what AI believes will be the most transformative:

Healthcare and Life Sciences

- **Diagnostics and imaging**: AI-driven radiology, pathology, and genomics tools will detect diseases earlier and more accurately.
- **Drug discovery**: AI models will design molecules, dramatically speeding up R&D cycles.
- **Personalized medicine**: AI will enable treatments tailored to individual genetics and health data.
- **Healthcare administration**: Automation of billing, coding, and records management.

Impact: Increased efficiency, lower costs, and better outcomes, but with heightened ethical and regulatory scrutiny

Finance and Insurance

- **Algorithmic trading**: AI models already dominate trading floors but will get even faster and more predictive.
- **Fraud detection**: AI will evolve to spot complex fraud patterns in real time.
- **Risk assessment and underwriting**: Insurers will use AI to more precisely calculate individual risk profiles.
- **Personalized financial services**: Robo-advisors will become even more sophisticated, managing investments and retirement planning.

Impact: Lower barriers to financial services, but potential risks around systemic bias and flash crashes

Manufacturing and Supply Chain

- **Smart factories**: Predictive maintenance, quality control via computer vision, and fully autonomous production lines.
- **Supply chain optimization**: AI will forecast demand, optimize logistics, and react in real time to disruptions.
- **Mass customization**: Tailoring manufacturing for individual customer preferences using AI-driven design.

Impact: Cost savings, more customization, and fewer but more technical jobs

Transportation and Logistics

- **Autonomous vehicles**: Trucks, taxis, and delivery vehicles will increasingly drive themselves.

- **Air traffic management**: AI will optimize routing, reduce delays, and increase airspace efficiency.
- **Logistics and warehousing**: Fully automated inventory, drone deliveries, and predictive route optimization.

Impact: Massive efficiency gains, but regulatory and public trust hurdles for autonomous mobility

Education and Learning

- **Personalized learning**: AI will deliver adaptive curriculums tuned to each student's learning style and pace.
- **Automated tutoring and grading**: Scalable support for students and teachers.
- **Upskilling and reskilling platforms**: AI-driven course recommendations based on career goals and market needs.

Impact: Wider access to quality education, but disruption to traditional schooling models

Retail and Consumer Services

- **Hyper-personalization**: AI will tailor product recommendations, marketing, and pricing to individuals.
- **Automated customer service**: Conversational AI will handle complex customer interactions.
- **Inventory management**: Predictive analytics will eliminate stockouts and overstocks.

Impact: Enhanced customer experiences, but job displacement in traditional retail roles

Media, Entertainment, and Content Creation

- **Generative AI**: Movies, music, games, and books partially or wholly created by AI.
- **Personalized content**: Streaming services and news feeds dynamically tailored in real time.
- **Deepfake technologies**: Opportunities for new entertainment forms, and serious risks around misinformation.

Impact: New creative possibilities, but ethical and authenticity challenges

Legal and Professional Services

- **Document drafting and review**: AI will draft contracts, analyze case law, and prepare filings.
- **Litigation prediction**: Models will assess the probability of case outcomes.
- **IP and compliance management**: Automating monitoring and enforcement.

Impact: Faster and cheaper legal work, but possible stratification between high-end advisory services and commoditized tasks

Energy and Utilities

- **Grid management**: AI will forecast energy demand and dynamically balance grids.
- **Renewable energy**: AI will optimize the deployment and operation of solar, wind, and storage.
- **Exploration and production**: Smarter resource identification in oil, gas, and mining.

Impact: Cleaner, more efficient energy systems, but tension between traditional and green energy sectors

Public Sector and Defense

- **Smart cities**: AI will drive traffic control, energy management, public safety, and service delivery.
- **Military applications**: Surveillance, cyber-defense, autonomous systems, and decision support.
- **Regulatory compliance**: AI will help governments monitor compliance with regulations faster.

Impact: Improved efficiency – but also rising concerns about surveillance and power centralization

Industries Facing Redefinition

Some sectors may be completely disrupted, including

- **Advertising** (with AI-created campaigns and ad buying)
- **Hospitality and Travel** (AI-curated experiences, robotic staff)
- **Agriculture** (precision farming with AI predicting crop yields and pest outbreaks)
- **Real Estate** (AI predicting market shifts, virtual property tours)

Overarching Themes Across All Industries

- **Job displacement + creation**: Automation will kill some jobs but create others, mostly needing higher skill levels.
- **Regulation**: The pace of AI governance will critically shape how (and how quickly) industries adapt.

- **Ethics and trust**: Industries that move faster than societal acceptance may face backlash.
- **IP and data ownership**: Who owns the models, training data, and outputs will become fiercely contested.

Will all of these industries be completely transformed? Ray Kurzweil, author of *The Singularity Is Nearer*, and many others hailing from the big tech companies seem to agree, in general. Sam Altman has long advocated for some type of universal basic income because of this job displacement. But what does that mean for predicting where humans will be needed, how jobs will change, and what new skills will be in demand? Many are predicting a surge in the trades and hands-on services. This trend has already been underway as the value of a college education relative to its cost has been under attack for some years as young people struggle to pay off student loans with degrees that are no longer considered high value in society. This means young people may want to better understand what will have high human value in the future and become an expert or master of that trade or service. Those who can master skills, judgment, knowledge, or expertise will be high value where those who were often a metaphorical cog in the machine may find themselves without a place in the workforce. This also includes a solid, if not advanced, understanding of how to use AI.

Hard work and dedication to your craft will become more important than ever. Mediocrity will be replaced with superior AI. But expert and skilled humans will become more valuable. This means our system will value merit. Much of this has happened before. The industries ripe for disruption with AI have already been through transformation between 2000 and 2025.

How Does the AI Disruption Compare to the Internet Disruption?

AI may *now* come for some of these industries in a way the internet did not, especially heavy manufacturing (robotics + AI) and agriculture (autonomous farming). In other words, AI might reach sectors the internet could only lightly touch.

Comparing the Digital Transformation

Heavily Disrupted by the Internet	Minimally Disrupted by the Internet
Retail (ecommerce, direct-to-consumer)	**Heavy Manufacturing** (cars, airplanes, machinery)
Media and Entertainment (streaming, user-generated content)	**Construction and Skilled Trades** (building homes, plumbing, HVAC)
Travel and Hospitality (online booking, peer-to-peer rentals)	**Utilities** (power, water, gas delivery systems)
Advertising and Marketing (digital ads, data-driven targeting)	**Primary Agriculture (smallholder farms)**
Financial Services (online banking, fintech, mobile payments)	**High-End Personal Services** (luxury spas, custom tailoring)
Education (e-learning, MOOCs, remote classes)	**Oil, Gas, and Mining** (physical extraction, refining)
Healthcare (Patient-Facing) (telemedicine, online info access)	**High-Stakes Advisory Services** (complex legal, surgical, financial expertise)

(*continued*)

Heavily Disrupted by the Internet	Minimally Disrupted by the Internet
Real Estate Transactions (online listings, virtual tours)	**Logistics and Freight (Physical Movement)** (ships, trucks, planes)
Recruitment and Employment (job boards, remote work platforms)	**Funeral Services** (localized, human-driven services)
Public Sector Services (e-government, digital taxes, online voting reg.)	

Looking back, the internet era deeply transformed certain sectors while leaving others relatively untouched. Media, retail, finance, logistics, and customer service saw massive upheaval as digital tools replaced physical infrastructure, automated workflows, and created entirely new business models. Yet many roles, especially those rooted in physical presence, skilled labor, or deeply human interaction were only moderately impacted. Electricians, plumbers, massage therapists, chefs, and frontline hospitality staff weren't made obsolete by the internet. The same may be true with AI: the minimally disrupted then could remain minimally disrupted, while others undergo seismic shifts, though it is likely that eventually every industry will be disrupted by AI and robotics.

Importantly, any industry that relies on physical presence or capital infrastructure may see its back-end functions transformed, but the front-end service delivery will remain deeply human. Consider hospitality. AI can help optimize bookings, tailor marketing offers, and predict staffing needs, but the actual experience of checking into a resort, enjoying a fine meal, or receiving a spa treatment still hinges on human service, attention to detail, and a welcoming environment. Airbnb disrupted the *booking* process and democratized hospitality, but it didn't remove the need for someone to clean, manage, and maintain the property. Nor did it erase the zoning, insurance, or customer service complexities that require human oversight. Now offering experiences, they understand the future will be in human experiences and how to deliver those.

In other sectors, particularly medicine, law, finance, business strategy, and high-end sales, the rise of AI will likely reinforce the value of experts rather than replace them. These fields often rely on deeply contextual thinking, trusted relationships, and years of honed judgment. Yes, AI may take on the grunt work: scanning contracts, preparing financial models, or identifying treatment pathways. But the final mile of delivery of professional services, the interpretation, the recommendation, the counsel, still requires human intelligence, empathy, and accountability.

This is especially true in what economists call the *experience economy*. As AI and automation take over functional tasks, people will increasingly seek out services and experiences that feel personal, bespoke, and emotionally engaging. Whether it's a wellness retreat, a sommelier-led tasting, a tailored investment strategy, or a custom legal consultation, value creation will increasingly depend on delivering something machines can't replicate: human connection.

Luxury, in particular, also remains grounded in physical and emotional presence. A five-star spa, a Michelin-star restaurant, or a private coaching session cannot exist in the cloud. They require space, ambiance, service, and skill, things that still live in the domain of people and place. The more AI advances, the more those who offer distinctive, high-touch, human experiences will be in demand. As automation becomes ubiquitous, *meaningful* human interactions become a premium product.

So while AI will transform workflows, eliminate inefficiencies, and rewire organizational structures, it will not erase the need for human labor, it will simply redefine where and how that labor creates value. Leaders must stop asking "what jobs will AI replace?" and start asking "what human strengths will become most valuable?" Organizations that blend human skill with AI augmentation, rather than seeking to substitute one for the other, will be the ones that thrive.

And in the midst of all this disruption, a fundamental truth remains: the final mile of value, whether in service, strategy, or experience, is still traveled by a human. Those with exceptional skills, experience, judgment, or abilities to connect and relate at a human level will thrive, and those caught in the middle may have trouble finding work.

Further, from a branding perspective the fundamentals of creating intellectual assets of value will become increasingly important. Trademarks are an indicator of trust and relationship with the customer. Will brands, brand value, and the trademarks that protect them be more valuable in the future? Perhaps, but patents and trade secrets will continue to protect the technology that drives research and development. This is the important component of AI and IP by defining who owns both human intelligence and machine-generated intelligence.

Key Takeaways

- **AI is accelerating disruption**: Once thought distant, the effects on knowledge work and organizational structures are happening now.
- **Cognitive work is shifting**: Repetitive white-collar tasks are increasingly automated, making human discernment and judgment premium skills.
- **Blue-collar and service jobs will be next**: Robotics combined with AI will extend disruption into warehouses, kitchens, factories, and retail.
- **Transparency will be demanded**: Organizations that conceal AI's role in outputs risk eroding trust with clients, regulators, and employees.
- **Leadership must evolve**: Managing AI systems alongside human teams requires new governance frameworks and strategies.

- **Experience economy resilience**: High-touch, personalized, and relationship-driven services will remain deeply human and highly valuable.
- **Human expertise is the differentiator**: Trusted advisors, skilled trades, and mastery-based professions will command premium value in the AI age.
- **Historical lessons apply**: Just as the internet revolution left some industries largely intact, AI will bypass certain physical, localized, or highly relational work – but may transform others that previously escaped disruption.
- **Innovation will be sector wide**: Healthcare, finance, education, manufacturing, and logistics will undergo profound AI-driven reinvention.
- **Future value lies in synthesis**: Success will come from blending human creativity and judgment with machine efficiency, not treating them as substitutes.

CHAPTER 9

Key Takeaways and the Road Ahead

We are not standing at the edge of another incremental innovation. We are at the dawn of a new age, the AI era. Unlike the industrial revolution, which mechanized muscle, or the digital revolution, which networked information, this transformation reaches into the essence of human cognition. Intelligence itself, the ability to reason, to learn, to create, is now a resource that can be engineered, replicated, and owned. The implications are staggering.

Those who understand how to use AI wisely will thrive. They will build organizations and societies that grow stronger, smarter, and more adaptive. But those who have lost the ability to think critically, numbed by algorithmic feeds, may find themselves left behind, first confined to manual work, then later displaced by machines that can perform it better, faster, and without fatigue.

When social media first emerged, its creators did not announce that it could harm mental health, fragment attention, or polarize entire nations by trapping users inside algorithmic echo chambers. They promised connection but delivered addiction.

What was meant to build community often spread comparison, outrage, and division.

J. C. Wolfe and N. E. Cronin, *Owning Intelligence*,
https://doi.org/10.1007/979-8-8688-2388-6_9

Today, many spend most of their waking hours scrolling through highly filtered and manipulated social media or living inside virtual gaming worlds, consuming news, opinions, and identity through the lens of a feed. This dependency on the digital mirror is shaping how we think, what we believe, and even how we define truth. It is the first great warning of what happens when technology evolves faster than our collective ability to manage it.

Artificial intelligence carries the same paradox: extraordinary promise coupled with equally profound peril. The companies leading this revolution are not warning us about what happens when millions lose their sense of purpose through work or productivity or when human creativity becomes indistinguishable from machine output.

As AI thinks, speaks, and acts with a semblance of sentience and shows empathy to hook us in conversation, we are entering a moral and economic frontier that demands new kinds of leadership, leaders who recognize that intelligence itself, once humanity's greatest advantage, is now becoming our greatest shared responsibility.

Those who choose to understand AI, not as magic but as a new form of capital, can redefine what success means. For IP professionals and organizational leaders, this is the frontier of ownership itself. In the AI era, the question is no longer just who owns the patent or the brand, but who owns the intelligence that powers them both.

Success will not be driven by coders alone, particularly since AI interfaces allow for everyone to participate in creating. It will require thoughtful stewards, executives, policymakers, and ethicists, who can build systems of trust, design governance for machines that learn, and ensure that humans remain not just relevant but essential. Ethical dilemmas will proliferate society: Can AI be your accountant, lawyer, or doctor? Could an AI lead a nation or command an army? Should it? The answers will depend on how wisely we manage the partnership between human and machine. The convergence of human judgment and trustworthy AI is not the destination, but the first step in a new evolution of intelligence.

Beyond the boundaries of business, a deeper cultural divide may be forming. Those with the skills or resources to think critically will navigate the AI world with agency and advantage. They can build businesses with fewer resources. Others may retreat into escapism, immersed in social media, games, and virtual realities where algorithms offer the illusion of control. Meritocracy will reward capability, while subsidies may sustain dependency.

This book has not attempted to resolve every social question that follows. Its purpose is more immediate and practical, to help leaders prepare their organizations for the shift already underway. The task now is to operationalize the idea of owning intelligence, to build the frameworks, policies, and cultures that equip people to thrive in the AI era. This is not a technical exercise, but a philosophical one, rooted in human responsibility and human engagement. The future belongs to those who understand both.

The Ethics of Owning Intelligence

The concept of *owning intelligence* raises profound ethical and philosophical questions about the boundaries between human creativity and artificial assistance. When an individual uses AI to generate a persona, create a movie, compose music, paint a digital masterpiece, or write a novel, the output reflects a hybrid process, part human intention, part machine execution. The human provides the direction, the taste, the emotional context, and the conceptual framing. The AI translates that input into a tangible form through pattern recognition, data synthesis, and algorithmic recombination.

In this sense, the individual who guides the AI is not so different from a conductor leading an orchestra or an actor interpreting a script. The artistry lies in the orchestration, the unique approach to prompting, the iterative refinement, and the vision to turn raw machine potential into expressive human meaning.

However, ethical complexities arise in determining ownership and authenticity. If a human artist develops a unique method of prompting an AI to produce consistent, high-quality creative works, should that process itself be considered proprietary intellectual property? Does authorship still belong to the person who conceived the idea or to the algorithm that produced the form? And what of the datasets that underpin these creations; if the AI draws upon existing copyrighted works, can any new creation truly be said to be "original"? These questions mirror past debates in art and technology, from the invention of photography to digital sampling in music, but they take on new urgency when the "artist" may be partly non-human.

The same ethical tension extends to invention and discovery. A scientist or engineer using AI to simulate molecular interactions or generate patentable designs is still exercising human ingenuity, but through a new medium. The individual might not physically build the prototype, yet the act of conceptualizing the question, framing the parameters, and interpreting the result represents intellectual labor. In this light, using AI to uncover or discover innovation is not unlike using a microscope or a telescope, an extension of human cognition.

What differentiates this era is that the tool is now intelligent, capable of contributing ideas, testing hypotheses, and even improving itself. We continue to witness advancements in the AI tools that further blur the lines between what the human and the machine have created. As AI tools train on content created by humans, eventually it may be difficult to distinguish between machine generated and human writing. Thus, the ethics of owning intelligence revolve not only around credit and control but also around the moral responsibility of creators who now share agency with machines. The challenge ahead lies in ensuring that as we invent with intelligence, we also safeguard the essence of human authorship, accountability, and creativity. Much will change in the future legal landscape, particularly in the ownership of intellectual property. Business leaders must stay attuned to the changes and consider the ethical implications as they build their roadmaps for the future.

Roadmap for Boards and Leaders

The AI era will reward organizations that not only innovate but also govern wisely. Owning intelligence is not a concept; it is a capability built through deliberate strategy, disciplined process, and ethical foresight.

This roadmap outlines how leaders can translate vision into action: by defining ownership and intellectual property strategy, establishing oversight mechanisms, preparing the workforce for profound shifts, anticipating societal and economic impacts, and maintaining adaptability amid constant change.

AI oversight is not a siloed compliance exercise but an enterprise-wide governance imperative. Anchored in legal leadership, supported by cross-functional collaboration, and guided by process discipline, it becomes the foundation for responsible innovation, risk mitigation, and long-term advantage.

1. **Define ownership and IP strategy**: Treat AI models, data, and outputs as core strategic assets. Establish clear policies on who owns training data, model weights, prompts, and generated outputs. Integrate AI-related IP into corporate valuation and M&A strategy. Audit contracts and vendor relationships for data rights and ensure that ownership is legally protected and operationally enforced.

2. **Build oversight mechanisms**: Create governance structures that ensure transparency, accountability, and ethical decision-making. Form AI oversight or risk committees that report directly to the board. Implement model documentation standards, audit trails, and vendor assessment frameworks. Require third-party explainability reports and testing protocols for bias, reliability, and data lineage.

3. **Integrate ethical and legal guardrails**: Embed ethical principles and legal compliance into the full AI lifecycle, from model selection to deployment. Adopt frameworks aligned with NIST, ISO, and OECD guidance. Establish cross-functional review processes involving legal, compliance, IT, HR, and operations. This ensures responsible innovation while maintaining public trust and regulatory readiness.

4. **Prepare for workforce shifts**: Identify functions most vulnerable to automation and develop proactive reskilling and redeployment strategies. Invest in continuous learning programs that enhance human capabilities, critical thinking, creativity, leadership, and empathy. Recognize that while roles will disappear, new ones will emerge around prompt engineering, AI governance, and human-AI collaboration. Do your best to project what will happen in your industry and plan ahead.

5. **Secure data and protect privacy**: Data remains the lifeblood of AI. Your proprietary knowledge, embedded in digital data, can be a secret weapon in the AI era. Build robust data governance frameworks that safeguard confidentiality, ensure quality, and prevent misuse. Establish protocols for anonymization, consent, and cross-border data transfer. Align with emerging data protection regulations and ethical standards for AI-driven decision-making.

6. **Anticipate social and economic impacts**: Recognize that AI adoption will reshape not only business models but also the social fabric around them. Address potential inequalities through inclusive hiring, community investment, and transparent communication about automation's impact. And monitor for AI bias that can tilt the scales in undesirable directions. Reputation and resilience depend on ensuring that technological progress benefits more than the bottom line.

7. **Stay adaptive**: Governance cannot be static. Establish review cycles for AI policies, conduct scenario planning exercises, and build resilience through stress-testing and horizon scanning. Encourage a culture of curiosity, accountability, and adaptability across all levels of leadership. Educate yourself, and educate your employees to stay ahead of the constantly evolving AI landscape.

8. **Foster collaboration and industry alignment**: Engage in industry consortia, standards development, and public-private partnerships to shape best practices. No single organization can navigate the ethical, legal, and technical complexities of AI alone. Collaboration enhances credibility and reduces systemic risk.

AI oversight is not a siloed compliance exercise but an enterprise-wide governance challenge.

We are all in this together, researching, learning, and exploring the unknown terrain of the AI era. The potential peril is too great to just hope that one group or another or one company will have all the answers.

We need a lot of smart people thinking about these issues, offering ideas, engaging in thoughtful exchanges and evolving thought leadership to protect humanity. Academics are racing to publish their peer-reviewed papers. The major consulting firms are flooding the market with polished PowerPoint decks on AI system implementation or newly coded work flows. Entrepreneurs are rebranding themselves overnight as AI governance experts to attract venture capital. Boutique consultancies are launching more nuanced and niche support across industry sectors. Conferences are multiplying, each promising the next great insight. The noise is deafening, but the truth is simple: the information already exists, and AI itself can now find it, synthesize it, and deliver it to anyone who knows how to ask the right questions.

The real differentiator is not access to information, but the ability to apply judgment, to exercise executive function. The leaders who will succeed are those who can discern where they are, envision where they need to go, and mobilize the right people to get there. Traditional credentials will fade in relevance. The new currency is critical thinking, adaptability, and the skillful use of AI to amplify human capability.

In this moment of transformation, wisdom and agility matter more than scale. The AI era will not be won by the biggest, but by the most adaptive, the ones who know how to think, to govern, and to own intelligence.

References

We have provided reference notes from the first instance of appearance by chapter. Some references may have been used in multiple chapters or incorporated into other areas of this book.

Chapter 2

A Proposal for the Dartmouth Summer Research Project on Artificial Intelligence. (n.d.). Stanford University. Retrieved from `https://www-formal.stanford.edu/jmc/history/dartmouth/dartmouth.html`

Tatnall, A. (Ed.). (2010). Ethics: The past, present and future of socio-technical systems design. In *History of computing: Learning from the past* (pp. 189–197). Springer. `https://doi.org/10.1007/978-3-642-15199-6_19`

The origins of artificial intelligence. August 15, 2023. ProboAI. Retrieved from `https://www.proboai.com/early-pioneers-ai-alan-turing`

University of Bristol. (2008). *Bristol researchers on early computing* [Press release]. Retrieved from `https://www.bristol.ac.uk/news/2008/212017945378.html`

J. C. Wolfe and N. E. Cronin, *Owning Intelligence*,
https://doi.org/10.1007/979-8-8688-2388-6

Chapter 3

A Media Operator. (May 2025). *Collective licensing wants to help publishers scrape back revenue from AI companies.* Retrieved from https://www.amediaoperator.com/analysis/collective-licensing-ai-pls-cla-copyright/

AP News. (January 15, 2025). *Google signs deal with AP to deliver up-to-date news through its Gemini AI chatbot.* Associated Press. https://apnews.com/article/0b57bcf8c80dd406daa9ba916adacfaf

Authors Guild. (December 12, 2024). *AI licensing for authors: Who owns the rights and what's a fair split?* https://authorsguild.org/news/ai-licensing-for-authors-who-owns-the-rights-and-whats-a-fair-split/

Authors Guild. (November 19, 2024). *HarperCollins' AI licensing deal: What authors need to know.* https://authorsguild.org/news/harpercollins-ai-licensing-deal/

Digiday. (July 10, 2025). *Condé Nast and Hearst strike Amazon AI licensing deals for Rufus.* https://digiday.com/media/conde-nast-and-hearst-strike-amazon-ai-licensing-deals-for-rufus/

Digiday. (December 27, 2024). *2024 in review: A timeline of the major deals between publishers and AI companies.* https://digiday.com/media/2024-in-review-a-timeline-of-the-major-deals-between-publishers-and-ai-companies/

Press Gazette. (November 4, 2025). *Who's suing AI and who's signing: Getty signs with Perplexity, Penske Media sues Google over AI Overviews.* https://pressgazette.co.uk/platforms/news-publisher-ai-deals-lawsuits-openai-google/

Straits Times. (June 10, 2025). *Academic publishers sign AI deals as Trump cuts research funding.* https://www.straitstimes.com/world/united-states/academic-publishers-sign-ai-deals-as-trump-cuts-research-funding/

TechTarget. (May 29, 2025). *The New York Times in multiyear licensing deal with Amazon. SearchEnterpriseAI.* https://www.techtarget.com/searchenterpriseai/news/366624903/The-New-York-Times-in-multiyear-licensing-deal-with-Amazon

The Atlantic. (June 25, 2025). *The end of publishing as we know it.* https://www.theatlantic.com/technology/archive/2025/06/generative-ai-pirated-articles-books/683009/

The Times. (December 2, 2024). *AI licensing deals can protect good journalism, says Reuters chief.* https://www.thetimes.co.uk/article/ai-licensing-deals-can-protect-good-journalism-says-reuters-chief-kgxjqstjw

Wired. (December 21, 2023). *Journalists Had No Idea about OpenAI's Deal To Use Their Stories.* https://www.wired.com/story/openai-axel-springer-news-licensing-deal-whats-in-it-for-writers/

Chapter 4

Batool, A., Zowghi, D., & Bano, M. (2023). Responsible AI governance: A systematic literature review. *Cornell University. Responsible AI Governance: A Systematic Literature Review*

Brundage, M., Avin, S., Clark, J., Toner, H., Eckersley, P., Garfinkel, B., Dafoe, A., Scharre, P., Zeitzoff, T., Filar, B., Cili, F., Trask, A., Carlsmith, J., Krueger, G., Maharaj, T., & Anderljung, M. (2018). *The malicious use of artificial intelligence: Forecasting, prevention, and mitigation.* University of Oxford. 1802.07228

Deloitte. (March 28, 2025). *4 steps to board AI oversight: Balancing risk and innovation. The Wall Street Journal (Sponsored Report). 4 Steps to Board AI Oversight: Balancing Risk and Innovation - WSJ*

European Commission. (2021). *Proposal for a regulation laying down harmonised rules on artificial intelligence (Artificial Intelligence Act).* Publications Office of the European Union.

Gasser, U., & Almeida, V. A. F. (2017). A layered model for AI governance. *IEEE Internet Computing, 21*(6), 58–62. https://doi.org/10.1109/MIC.2017.4180835

Giffen, B. van. (2023). *How boards of directors govern artificial intelligence.* ICANN / AIS eLibrary / The Australian. "How Boards of Directors Govern Artificial Intelligence" by Benjamin van Giffen and Helmuth Ludwig

Harvard Law School Forum on Corporate Governance. (September 17, 2024). *Board oversight of AI. Board Oversight of AI*

Mueller, M. L. (2025). *Declaring independence in cyberspace.* Tech Policy Press.

OECD principles on artificial intelligence. Organisation for Economic Co-operation and Development. AI principles | OECD

Kapur, Akash. *Can the Internet be governed?* The New Yorker. (2024). The Search for a New and Better Internet | The New Yorker

Whittaker, M., Alper, M., Crawford, K., Dobbe, R., Kaziunas, L., Mathur, V., Mulligan, D., Raji, I. D., & Richardson, R. (2018). *AI Now Report 2018.* AI Now Institute.

World Economic Forum. (2024). *Governance in the Age of Generative AI: A 360 Approach for Resilient Policy and Regulation,* World Economic Forum.

Zhang, B., Dafoe, A., & Whittlestone, J. (2019). *AI governance: A research agenda.* Centre for the Governance of AI, University of Oxford.

Google

Google. (2023). *Our responsible approach to building guardrails for generative AI.* https://blog.google/technology/ai/our-responsible-approach-to-building-guardrails-for-generative-ai/

Google. (2025). *AI protection: Security for the AI era.* https://cloud.google.com/blog/products/identity-security/introducing-ai-protection-security-for-the-ai-era

Google. (2024). *Gemini app policy guidelines.* https://gemini.google/policy-guidelines/

Google. (2024). *Gemini for Google Cloud and responsible AI.* https://cloud.google.com/gemini/docs/discover/responsible-ai

Google. (2024). *Guardrails API | Checks.* https://developers.google.com/checks/guide/ai-safety/guardrails

Google. (2024). *Safety guidance | Gemini API.* https://ai.google.dev/gemini-api/docs/safety-guidance

Google. (2024). *Safeguard your models | Responsible Generative AI Toolkit.* https://ai.google.dev/responsible/docs/safeguards

Google. (February 2025). *Responsible AI progress report.* https://ai.google/static/documents/ai-responsibility-update-published-february-2025.pdf

Microsoft

Microsoft. (June 2022). *Responsible AI Standard: Microsoft's framework for building AI systems responsibly.* https://blogs.microsoft.com/on-the-issues/2022/06/21/microsofts-framework-for-building-ai-systems-responsibly/

Microsoft. (October 2023). *Microsoft's AI safety policies.* https://blogs.microsoft.com/on-the-issues/2023/10/26/microsofts-ai-safety-policies/

Microsoft. (April 2024). *How Microsoft discovers and mitigates evolving attacks against AI guardrails.* https://www.microsoft.com/en-us/security/blog/2024/04/11/how-microsoft-discovers-and-mitigates-evolving-attacks-against-ai-guardrails/

Microsoft. (2024). *Building AI responsibly.* https://www.microsoft.com/en-us/microsoftacts/building-ai-responsibly

Microsoft. (2024). *Creating effective security guardrails with metaprompt/system.* https://techcommunity.microsoft.com/blog/azure-ai-foundry-blog/marchresponsibly-creating-effective-security-guardrails-with-metapromptsystem-me/4099284

Microsoft. (2024). *Default guardrails and controls for Azure AI Foundry models.* https://learn.microsoft.com/en-us/azure/ai-foundry/foundry-models/concepts/default-safety-policies

Microsoft. (2024). *Responsible AI in Azure Machine Learning.* https://learn.microsoft.com/en-us/azure/machine-learning/concept-responsible-ai

Microsoft. (2024). *Responsible AI: Ethical policies and practices.* https://www.microsoft.com/en-us/ai/responsible-ai

Microsoft. (2024). *Responsible AI: Principles and approach.* https://www.microsoft.com/en-us/ai/principles-and-approach

Microsoft. (2024). *Responsible generative AI development on Windows.* https://learn.microsoft.com/en-us/windows/ai/rai

OpenAI, Anthropic, and AWS

Anthropic. (May 2024). *Updating our Usage Policy.* https://www.anthropic.com/news/updating-our-usage-policy

Anthropic. (August 2025). *Usage Policy update.* https://www.anthropic.com/news/usage-policy-update

AWS. (January 2025). *AWS Responsible AI Policy.* Amazon Web Services, Inc. https://aws.amazon.com/ai/responsible-ai/policy/

OpenAI. (2025). *Creating images and videos in line with our policies.* https://openai.com/policies/creating-images-and-videos-in-line-with-our-policies/

OpenAI. (October 2025). *Usage policies.* https://openai.com/policies/usage-policies/

Meta and xAI

Meta. (2024). *Connect 2024: The responsible approach we're taking to generative AI.* `https://ai.meta.com/blog/responsible-ai-connect-2024/`

Meta. (2024). *Seamless Use Policy.* `https://ai.meta.com/resources/models-and-libraries/seamless-use-policy/`

Meta. (April 2024). *Our approach to labeling AI-generated content and manipulated media.* About Facebook. `https://about.fb.com/news/2024/04/metas-approach-to-labeling-ai-generated-content-and-manipulated-media/`

Meta. (February 2025). *Meta says it may stop development of AI systems it deems too risky: Frontier AI Framework.* TechCrunch.

Chapter 5

Bankins, S., Molloy, C., & Tiernan, S. (2023). *A multilevel review of artificial intelligence in organizations. Journal of Organizational Behavior.*

Board of Governors of the Federal Reserve System. (2021). *Artificial intelligence and machine learning in financial services.* Washington, D.C. Speech by Governor Brainard on supporting responsible use of AI and equitable outcomes in financial services - Federal Reserve Board

Zuiderveen Borgesius, F. J. (2020). Strengthening legal protection against discrimination by algorithms and artificial intelligence. *The International Journal of Human Rights, 24*(10), 1572–1593. `https://doi.org/10.1080/13642987.2020.1743976`

Brundage, M., Avin, S., Clark, J., et al. (2018). *The malicious use of artificial intelligence: Forecasting, prevention, and mitigation.* Oxford University.

Carnegie Mellon University. (2025). *AI builds trust in knowledge work through real-time feedback* (Tepper School of Business Research Spotlight). New Research Explores How AI Can Build Trust in Knowledge Work | Tepper School of Business

Cihon, P., Maas, M. M., & Kemp, L. (2020). Should artificial intelligence governance be centralised? Design lessons from history. *Technology in Society, 67,* 101728.

Gasser, U., & Almeida, V. A. F. (2017). A layered model for AI governance. *IEEE Internet Computing, 21*(6), 58–62.

Hagendorff, T. (2020). The ethics of AI ethics: An evaluation of guidelines. *Minds and Machines, 30,* 99–120.

Jobin, A., Ienca, M., & Vayena, E. (2019). The global landscape of AI ethics guidelines. *Nature Machine Intelligence, 1,* 389–399.

Murire, O. T., et al. (2024). Artificial intelligence and its role in shaping organizational work practices. *Administrative Sciences.*

Murire, O. T., et al. (2024). Artificial intelligence adoption: Cultural transformation and work practices. *Administrative Sciences.*

National Institute of Standards and Technology. (2023). *Artificial intelligence risk management framework (AI RMF 1.0).* U.S. Department of Commerce.

PASQUALE, F. (2020). *New Laws of Robotics: Defending Human Expertise in the Age of AI.* Harvard University Press. https://doi.org/10.2307/j.ctv3405w6p

PricewaterhouseCoopers. (2022). *Responsible AI: A framework for building trust.* PwC Global. Responsible AI - Maturing from theory to practice

Prunkl, C., et al. (2025). *Organization matters: A qualitative study of organizational dynamics in red teaming practices for generative AI* [arXiv preprint].

Schweitzer, S., Narayanan, D., McGuire, J., & De Cremer, D. (2025). Leading AI Adoption in Organizations: Introducing a Behavioral

Human-Centered Approach. *International Journal of Human–Computer Interaction*, 1–12. https://doi.org/10.1080/10447318.2025.2531287

Stouten, J., & Camps, J. (2024). *Employee well-being in the age of AI: Perceptions, concerns, behaviors, and outcomes* [arXiv preprint].

Ubellacker, Thomas. (2025). *Making sense of AI limitations: How individual perceptions shape organizational readiness* [arXiv preprint].

U.S. Chamber of Commerce. (2023). *Report on artificial intelligence regulation and oversight.* Washington, D.C. Artificial Intelligence Commission Report | U.S. Chamber of Commerce

Wang, M., et al. (2025). How and when artificial intelligence adoption promotes employee knowledge sharing? *Frontiers in Psychology.*

World Economic Forum. (2025). *Building trust in AI through a new global governance framework.* Geneva. How the world can build a global AI governance framework | World Economic Forum

Chapter 6

Lawyer Monthly (2025). *OpenEvidence Files Lawsuit Against Pathway Medical for Alleged Trade Secret Misappropriation.* Lawyer Monthly https://www.lawyer-monthly.com/2025/03/openevidence-files-lawsuit-against-pathway-medical-for-alleged-trade-secret-misappropriation/

Mihalopoulos, Dan (2025). *Syndicated content in Sun-Times special section included AI-generated misinformation* Chicago Sun-Times. https://chicago.suntimes.com/news/2025/05/20/syndicated-content-sunday-print-sun-times-ai-misinformation

Banks, Richard et al. (2025). *The Impact of Generative AI on Critical Thinking: Self-Reported Reductions in Cognitive Effort and Confidence Effects From a Survey of Knowledge Workers.* Microsoft https://www.microsoft.com/en-us/research/wp-content/uploads/2025/01/lee_2025_ai_critical_thinking_survey.pdf

US Patent and Trademark Office (2025). *Revised Inventorship Guidance for AI-Assisted Inventions.* Department of Commerce. https://public-inspection.federalregister.gov/2025-21457.pdf?utm_campaign=subscriptioncenter&utm_content=&utm_medium=email&utm_name=&utm_source=govdelivery&utm_term=

Kim, Charles et al. (2024). Inventorship guidance for AI-assisted Inventions. US Patent and Trademark Office https://www.uspto.gov/sites/default/files/documents/inventorship-guidance-for-ai-assisted-inventions.pdf

Chapter 7

Abbott, F. M. (2000). *Distributed governance at the WTO–WIPO: An emerging intellectual property paradigm for developing countries.* **Journal of International Economic Law, 3**(1), 63–81. https://doi.org/10.1093/jiel/3.1.63

Al-Busaidi, A. (2024). *Investigating the impact of generative artificial intelligence on copyrighted materials: A multi-perspective analysis.* ScienceDirect. https://www.sciencedirect.com/science/article/pii/S2444569X24001690

Bharati, P. (2024). *AI and intellectual property: Legal frameworks and future directions.* **Law Journal of India, 4**(2), 31–193.

Chesterman, S. (2025). *Intellectual property rights and generative AI.* **Policy and Society, 44**(1), 23–45. https://doi.org/10.1093/polsoc/psad001

Cuntz, A. (2023). *Artificial intelligence and intellectual property: An economic perspective* (WIPO Economic Research Working Paper No. 77). World Intellectual Property Organization. https://www.wipo.int/publications/en/details.jsp?id=4647

Edward Elgar Publishing. (April 2024). *AI and intellectual property: Navigating the future of innovation.* **Elgar Blog**. https://elgar.blog/2024/10/07/ai-and-intellectual-property-navigating-the-future-of-innovation/

Financial Times. (August 2025). *Who owns the copyright for AI work?* **Financial Times**. https://www.ft.com/content/74b1841f-bf57-4934-a06a-3611d61e4319?syn-25a6b1a6=1

Guardian. (February 2025). *Creative industries are among the UK's crown jewels – and AI is out to steal them.* **The Guardian**. https://www.theguardian.com/commentisfree/2025/feb/22/creative-industries-are-among-the-uks-crown-jewels-and-ai-is-out-to-steal-them

Gregory, H. (October 7, 2023). *AI and the role of the board of directors.* **The Harvard Law School Forum on Corporate Governance**. https://corpgov.law.harvard.edu/2023/10/07/ai-and-the-role-of-the-board-of-directors/

Matulionyte, V., & Lee, R. (2025). *Copyright in AI-generated works: Lessons from recent developments in patent law* (arXiv:2503.04738). arXiv. https://doi.org/10.48550/arXiv.2503.04738

Mishra, S. (April 2, 2025). *AI in focus in 2025: Boards and shareholders set their sights on AI.* **The Harvard Law School Forum on Corporate Governance**. https://corpgov.law.harvard.edu/2025/04/02/ai-in-focus-in-2025-boards-and-shareholders-set-their-sights-on-ai/

National Association of Corporate Directors. (2023). *Director essentials: AI and board governance.* NACD.

Nasdaq Governance Solutions. (2023). *2023 global governance pulse.* Nasdaq.

Nasdaq. (2023). *Digitizing governance: Exploring AI's transformational influence in the boardroom.* Nasdaq. https://www.nasdaq.com/solutions/governance/boardvantage

Novelli, L., Galli, F., & Marino, M. (2024). *Generative AI in EU law: Liability, intellectual property, privacy, and cybersecurity* (arXiv:2401.07348). arXiv. https://doi.org/10.48550/arXiv.2401.07348

Okediji, R. L. (2008). *WIPO-WTO relations and the future of global intellectual property.* **University of Minnesota Law School Faculty Articles**, 1896. https://scholarship.law.umn.edu/faculty_articles/1896

PC Gamer. (July 2025). *EU-commissioned study on generative AI and copyright suggests overturning the current opt-out approach.* **PC Gamer**. https://www.pcgamer.com/software/ai/eu-commissioned-study-on-generative-ai-and-copyright-suggests-overturning-the-current-opt-out-approach-that-effectively-treats-silence-as-consent/

Poland, B. (2023). *Generative AI and U.S. intellectual property law* (arXiv:2311.16023). arXiv. https://doi.org/10.48550/arXiv.2311.16023

Plotkin, R. (2024). *AI armor: Securing the future of your AI company with strategic intellectual property.* Unstoppable CEO Press.

Ramalho, A. (2024). *Intellectual property protection for AI-generated creations: Europe, the United States, Australia and Japan.* Routledge.

Reuters. (August 2025). *Newsrooms vs. neural nets: How courts are handling DMCA claims against GenAI.* **Reuters**. https://www.reuters.com/legal/legalindustry/newsrooms-vs-neural-nets-how-courts-are-handling-dmca-claims-against-genai-2025-08-27/

Scannell, B. (2024). *A critical analysis of the interaction between copyright law and artificial intelligence* (Doctoral dissertation, University College Cork). University College Cork.

Shah, R., Irpan, A., Turner, A. M., Wang, A., Conmy, A., Lindner, D., Brown-Cohen, J., Ho, L., Nanda, N., Popa, R. A., Jain, R., Greig, R., Albanie, S., Emmons, S., Farquhar, S., Krier, S., Rajamanoharan, S., Bridgers, S., Ijitoye, T.,... Dragan, A. (2025). *An approach to technical AGI safety and security.* Google DeepMind.

Srivastava, R. K. (2023). *Artificial intelligence and intellectual property laws: Prospects and challenges.* Independent Author.

Times. (June 2025). *Robot laws won't work without international co-operation.* **The Times**. https://www.thetimes.com/uk/law/article/robot-laws-wont-work-without-international-co-operation-jw3rv99s0

Wiener, G. (Ed.). (2024). *Intellectual property and artificial intelligence* (Opposing Viewpoints series). Greenhaven Publishing.

WIPO, & Swiss Federal Institute of Intellectual Property. (2023). *AI and IP: Theory to policy and back again – Policy and research recommendations at the intersection of artificial intelligence and intellectual property.* World Intellectual Property Organization. https://www.wipo.int/publications/en/details.jsp?id=4768

World Intellectual Property Organization (WIPO). (2024). *Generative artificial intelligence: Patent landscape report.* WIPO. https://doi.org/10.34667/tind.49740

World Intellectual Property Organization (WIPO). (2024). *Generative AI: Navigating intellectual property.* WIPO Conversation - AI Inventions

World Trade Organization (2025). *Trading with Intelligence: How Artificial Intelligence (AI) Shapes and is Shaped by International Trade.* https://mddb.apec.org/Documents/2025/MM/MRT/25_mrt_008.pdf

Chapter 8

Altman, S. (2021). *Moore's Law for Everything.* Substack. Retrieved from https://moores.samaltman.com/

Brynjolfsson, E., & McAfee, A. (2016). *The Second Machine Age: Work, Progress, and Prosperity in a Time of Brilliant Technologies.* New York: W.W. Norton & Company.

Ford, M. (2016). *Rise of the Robots: Technology and the Threat of a Jobless Future.* New York: Basic Books.

Frey, C. B., & Osborne, M. A. (2017). *The future of employment: How susceptible are jobs to computerisation?* Technological Forecasting and Social Change, 114, 254–280.

Kurzweil, R. (2005). *The Singularity Is Near: When Humans Transcend Biology.* New York: Viking.

Kurzweil, R. (2022). *The Singularity Is Nearer.* New York: Viking.

Manyika, J., Chui, M., Bughin, J., Dobbs, R., Bisson, P., & Marrs, A. (2013). *Disruptive technologies: Advances that will transform life, business, and the global economy*. McKinsey Global Institute. https://www.mckinsey.com/capabilities/tech-and-ai/our-insights/disruptive-technologies

Schwab, K. (2016). *The Fourth Industrial Revolution*. Geneva: World Economic Forum. https://www.weforum.org/about/the-fourth-industrial-revolution-by-klaus-schwab/

Tegmark, M. (2017). *Life 3.0: Being Human in the Age of Artificial Intelligence*. New York: Alfred A. Knopf.

Webb, A. (2019). *The Big Nine: How the Tech Titans and Their Thinking Machines Could Warp Humanity*. New York: PublicAffairs.

World Economic Forum. (2023). *Future of Jobs Report 2023*. Geneva: World Economic Forum.

General – Governance, Futurecasting, and Disruption

Ackerman, Evan, The Electronic Highway: How 1960s visionaries presaged today's autonomous vehicle, IEEE spectrum, August 2, 2016

Balasubramanian, Manikandan and Pramath Malik, In search of the next patent war, Intellectual Asset Management Magazine, June 1, 2015.

Banker, Steve, Will the autonomous truck race require greater simplicity, Forbes, September 1, 2019.

Batra, Neal, Betts, David, Davis, Steve, Force of change the Future of Health, Deloitte Insights, April 30, 2019.

Berman, Dennis and Jerry Wolfe, Big data's Promise, Peril, The Wall Street Journal, October 5, 2015.

Bhuiyan, Johana and Charlie Warzel, God View: Uber Investigates Its Top New York Executive For Privacy Violations, BuzzFeed, November 18, 2014.

Bloomberg Business Week, the Year Ahead Special Issue, October 28, 2019

Boorstin, Julia, Era of mega-funded, money losing unicorn startups is coming to an end, CNBC, January 23, 2020

Borland, Kelsi Maree, Do we have the infrastructure for driverless cars? Globe Street.com, December 13, 2018

Brown, Brad et al. Big data: The next frontier for innovation, competition and productivity, McKinsey & Company, 2011

Bucholz, Scott, Briggs, Bill, Deloitte Tech Trends 2020

Burgess, Matt, Wired explains What is the Internet of Things, Wired UK, February 16, 2018

Cadler, Simon, Gatwick airport drone shutdown could have been an inside job, Independent, September 27, 2019

Carrier, Ryan, Implementing Guidelines for Governance, Oversight of AI and Automation, Communications of the ACM, February 12, 2019

CB insights, 38 Ways drones will impact society: from fighting war to forecasting weather, UAVs change everything, Research Briefs, January 9, 2020.

Clifton, Brian, Successful Analytics: Gain Business Insights by Managing Google Analytics, Advanced Web Metrics, 2015.

Chapin, Lyman, Scott Eldridge, and Karen Rose, The Internet of Things: An Overview, The Internet Society, 2015.

Cheng, Roger, The 5G wireless revolution, explained, CNet, October 27, 2019

Chin, Josh, The Internet Divided Between the US and China, Has Become a Battleground, Wall Street Journal, February 9, 2019

Christian, Anderson, What to expect from virtual reality in the future? Thrive Global, November 19, 2019

CMO C-Suite Studies, From Stretched to Strengthened: Insights from the Global Chief Marketing Officer Study, IBM Corporation, 2011.

CNN Library, Enron Fast Facts, Last Updated April 24, 2019

Columbus, Louis, The Best Big Data and Business Analytics Companies to Work for In 2015, Forbes, May 9, 2015.

Cook, Tim, Tim Cook: TV, Cars, Watches and More, The Wall Street Journal, October 27, 2015.

Copeland, B.J. Artificial Intelligence, Encyclopedia Britannica,

Daniel, Tony, Makes the Case for Trust Busting Big Tech Companies, The Federalist, June 14, 2014.

Dastin, Jeffrey, Amazon scraps secret AI recruiting tool that showed bias again women, Reuters, October 9, 2018

Davis, Bob and FitzGerald, Drew, 5 G Future Ready, Wall Street Journal, February 4, 2020

Delooper, Christian, What is 5? Digital Trends, November 18, 2019

D'Onfro, Jillian, AI 50: America's most promising artificial intelligence companies, Forbes, September 17, 2019.

Dull, Tamara, A Non-Geek's Big Data Playbook, SAS Best Practices.

Dredge, Stuart, 91% of top brands have apps, but how many of them are any good?, The Guardian. October 28, 2011.

Duvall, Tyler, Hannon, Eric, Katseff, Jared, Safran, Ben and Wallace, Tyler, A New look at autonomous vehicle infrastructure, McKinsey & Company Resources, May 2019

Dwoskin, Elizabeth and Deepa Seetharaman, Facebook Restricts Access to Its Data Trove, The Wall Street Journal, September 21, 2015.

The Economist, White Paper by Toray, The future of healthcare, The Economist, 2017

Finely, Klint, The Wired Guide to Net Neutrality, Wired, May 9, 2018

Forbes Technology Council, 15 unexpected consequences of GDPR, Forbes, August 15, 2018

Forester, Jim, Weather creates challenges for next generation of vehicles, Forbes, November 22, 2019

Fraser, Ian, Five predictions for the future of money, Raconteur, March 15, 2019

Goldman, Jake and Ben Ilfeld, iOS 9 Content Blockers: Impact Analysis and Mitigating Strategies, 10up. September 23, 2015.

Garber, Jonathan, Housing market come back heats up, Fox Business News, November 27, 2019.

Gottfried, Miriam, How Cable Companies Can Capture the Mobile Internet, The Wall Street Journal, September 22, 2015.

Google Seeks Richer Role With Own Content, The Wall Street Journal, February 7, 2014.

Gorman, Megan, How millennials are revolutionizing the home buying process, Forbes, August 31, 2019

Graziano, Kent, The true impact of GDPR is emerging now, CIO Dive, May 20, 2019.

Guimarães, Thiago, Revealed: A Breakdown of the Demographics for Each of the Different Social Networks, Business Insider, January 23, 2015.

Hao, Karen, This is how AI bias really happens – and why it's so hard to fix, MIT Technology Review, February 4, 2019

Harder, Amy, Bill Gates faces daunting nuclear energy future, Axios, July 15, 2019

Hazlett, Thomas, The New Trustbusters Are coming for Big Tech, Reason, October 2019

Hendler, James, As governments adopt artificial intelligence, there's little oversight and lots of danger, Phys.org, April 18, 2019

Heppelmann, James and Michael Porter, "How Smart, Connected Products are Transforming Competition, Harvard Business Review, November 2014.

Hennigan, W.J., Experts say drones pose a national security threat and we aren't ready, Time, May 31, 2018

Hernbroth, Megan, The era of the unicorn may be on its way out in 2020, Business Insider December 6, 2019

Hirschauge, Orr and Deepa Seetharaman, Facebook Looks to Bring virtual Reality to Mobile Devices, The Wall Street Journal, July 29, 2015.

Hobson, Katherine, The case for a course of virtual reality, US News and World Report, September 4, 2019

Hoffower, Hillary, More millennials are ditching big US cities for the suburbs and it shows just how dire the unaffordable housing crisis is, Business Insider, September 27, 2019

Hoffower, Hillary, millennials are flooding into these 25 US cities to find good jobs and earn more money, Business Insider, December 23, 2019

Holt, Kris, Google CEO Sundar Pichai Says AI Needs to Be Regulated, Forbes, January 20, 2020

Huddleston, Cameron, Experts predict how long cash will survive, Go Banking Rates, January 24, 2019

Hruska, Joel, Self-driving cars still can't handle snow, rain or heavy weather, Extreme Tech, October 30, 2018.

Javanmardian, Minoo, Lingampally, Aditya, Can AI Address Health Care's Red Tape Problem, Harvard Business Review, November 5, 2018

Johnson, Eric, America desperately needs fiber internet, and the tech giants won't save us, Vox, January 10, 2019

Johansson, Anna, The internet is due for a split, here's what you need to know, The Next Web, October 4, 2018.

Kapadia, Shefali, Trade and tech push supply chains from global to local, Supply Chain Drive, September 5, 2018

Kapner, Suzanne, Data Pushes Aside Chief Merchants, The Wall Street Journal, September 20, 2015.

Khurana, Ryan, Artificial intelligence Needs Private Markets for Regulation - Here's Why, Observer, January 23, 2020

Key Challenges in Big Data, Gartner, August 17, 2018

Knight, Will, AI Is Biased. Here's How Scientists Are Trying to Fix It, Wired, December 19, 2019.

Kolodny, Lora, Former Google CEO predicts the internet will split in two - and one part will be led by China, CNBC, September 20, 2018

Kusisto, Laura, Housing Market gaining modest strength, indicators show, Wall Street Journal, October 29, 2019

Lloyd, Richard, The Rise of the Google Gorilla, Intellectual Asset Management Magazine, November 2015.

Laurie, Ron, Constructing a holistic corporate patent monetization strategy, Intellectual Asset Management Magazine, June 2015.

Law Library of Congress: Regulation of Artificial Intelligence in selected Jurisdictions, The Law library of Congress global Research Directorate, January 2019

Madrigal, Alexis, Waymo's Robots drove more miles than everyone else combined, The Atlantic, February 14, 2019.

Manyika, James, Silberg, Jake and Presten, Britttany, What do we do about the biases in AI?, Harvard Business Review, October 25, 2019

Marshall, Jack, Apple Propels Cottage Industry of Ad Blockers, The Wall Street Journal, September 24, 2015.

Martin, Nicole, Okay Google, will voice be the future of search?, Forbes, November 6, 2018

Marr, Bernard, The key definitions of artificial intelligence that explain its importance, Forbes, February 14, 2018

Matte, Daniel and Mccullagh, Kevin, Will Smartwatches Be a Hit?, The Wall Street Journal, May 10, 2015.

McKenna, Michael, Three notable examples of AI Bias, AI Business, October 14, 2019

McPharlin, Kelly, Why we should listen to Bill Gates on Nuclear Energy, NEI, February 4, 2019

Meola, Andrew, What is the internet of things? What IO means and how it works, Business Insider, May 10, 2018

Mire, Sam, What's the future of health care? 31 experts share their insights, Disruptor Daily, June 27, 2019

MIT Technology Review; Asia's AI Agenda, The ethics of AI, 2019

Morrison, Maureen, and Tim Peterson, The War on Advertising, Advertising Age, September 14, 2015.

Morrison, Maureen, The CMO's Guide to Messaging Apps, Advertising Age, September 14, 2015.

Morgan, Jacob, A simple explanation of the internet of things, Forbes, May 13, 2014

Mui, Chunka & Carroll, Paul B, The New Killer Apps: How Large Companies Can Out-Innovate Start Ups, Cornerloft Press, 2013.

Nellis, Stephen, Dastin, Jeffrey, Microsoft wants to erase its carbon footprint - past and future, Reuters, January 17, 2020.

Nelson, Raymond, The future of fiber, Forbes, April 18, 2018

Ngak, Chenda, As Google Fiber expands to Olathe, Kan., millions of Americans still offline, CBS News. 2013

Nusca, Andrew, Net Neutrality Explain What It Means and Why It Matters, Fortune, November 23, 2017

Oh, Soo Jin, Buyer Behavior Trends Driving the Digital Shift Toward Mobile, Marketing Land, June 17, 2015.

Oliver, Erik and Kent Richardson, The strategic counter-assertion model for patent portfolio RoI, Intellectual Asset Management Magazine, March 2015.

Oliver, Nick, Potocnik, Kristina and Calvard, Thomas, To Make Self Driving Cars Safe, We Also Need Better Roads and Infrastructure, Harvard Business Review, August 14, 2018

Peterson, Tim, Entertainments engineers: How video is being reprogrammed at YouTube, Advertising Age, September 15, 2015.

Powell, Jessica, The Problem is Bigger Than We Work, Why wall street Realized Unicorns Aren't so Magical, Time Magazine, November 21, 2019.

Primack, Dan, Elizabeth Warren's trust-busting plan eyes Silicon Valley mergers, Axios, March 11, 2019.

Robot Technology, Encyclopedia Britannica, last updated November 27, 2019

Rubin, Peter, Want to know the real future of AR/VR? Wired, August 5, 2019

Seetharaman, Deepa, Oculus Adds Movies and TV, The Wall Street Journal, September 24, 2015.

Schmidt, Ann, Millennials are moving to these affordable cities, Fox Business, October 3, 2019.

Segan, Sascha, What Is 5G? PC, January 2, 2020

Serwer, Andy with Zahn, Max, Why we should Celebrate the End of the Unicorn, Yahoo Finance, November 9, 2019.

Sharma, Amol and Shalini Ramachandran, HBO Explores the 'How' of Streaming Option, The Wall Street Journal, October 29, 2014.

Silberg, Jake, Manyika, Tackling bias in artificial intelligence and in humans, McKinsey Global Institute, June 2019

Simon, Matt, What is a robot? Wired, August 24, 107

Stamm, Stephanie, A Decade of Unicorns Ends With a Little Less Magic, Wall Street journal, December 17, 2019.

Stanford Encyclopedia of Philosophy, Artificial Intelligence, first published July 12, 2018

Stinson, Jim, Autonomous Trucking still Distant, Transport Topics, January 30, 2019

Supply Chain Quarterly Staff, Supply chains shift from global to local, Supply Chain Quarterly, Q3 2018.

Taulli, Tom, How Bias Distorts AI, Forbes, August 4, 2019

Tepper, Nona, Nearly two-thirds of B2B companies have mobile web sites and apps, Internet Retailer. July 31, 2015.

The Narrowing of the Open Web, Infographic Bloomberg Business Week October 28, 2019

Topol, Eric, Your Smartphone Will See You Now, The Wall Street Journal, January 9, 2015.

Tree, an MIT Research Project, active from January 2017 to June 2017. `https://www.media.mit.edu/projects/tree/overview/`

Verizon 2019 Data Breach Investigations Report

Vincent, James, Alphabet CEO Sundar Pichai says there is no question that AI needs to be regulated, The Verge, January 20, 2020

Vonck, Richard, Connecting with Our Connected World, The Futurist, World Future Society, 2013.

Varey, James, Wealthy Americans flee high tax states, take billions with them, Tax the rich, the rich leave, The Washington Times, April 10, 2019.

Wartzman, Rick, The Tricky Role of the CEO in a New Era of Social Responsibility, Wall Street Journal, December 12, 2019.

Webb, Amy how to Do Strategic Planning Like a Futurist, Future Today Institute July 30, 2019

Wharton Knowledge, Why cash won't lose its cachet anytime soon, Knowledge @ Wharton, May 23, 2019

With Big Data Comes Big Responsibility: An Interview with Alex 'Sandy' Pentland, Harvard Business Review., November 2014.

What will the future look like without net neutrality, WSJ Video, June 11, 2018. `https://www.wsj.com/video/what-will-the-future-look-like-without-net-neutrality/A5A2F482-065B-4529-B495-921CBFF77FF9.html`

Wolfe, Jennifer, Blockchain in the Boardroom, Create Space, 2018.

World Economic Forum Community Paper, Transforming Infrastructure: Frameworks for Bringing the Fourth Industrial Revolution to Infrastructure, Davos 2020.

World Economic Forum Insight Report in Collaboration with Boston Consulting Group, The Net Zero Challenge: Fast Forward to Decisive Climate Action, January 2020.

World Economic Forum Insight Report in Collaboration with Marsh & McLennan and Zurich Insurance Group, The Global Risks Report 2020, January 2020.

World Economic Forum Insight Report in Collaboration with FIDO Alliance, Passwordless Authentication The next breakthrough in secure digital transformation, January 2020.

Yonck, Richard, Scenario: Life with the Internet of Everything, The Futurist, World Future Society, November – December 2013.

99 Firms.com, 36 Key Voice Search Statistics You Can No Longer Ignore, April 16, 2019

Akhtar, Allana, 13 six figure jobs for people who value stability and career growth, Business Insider, August 15, 2019

Bethune, Sophie, Gen Z more likely to report mental health concerns, American Psychological Association, January 2019

Bulajewski, Mike The sharing economy was dead on arrival, Daily Jestor, December 12, 2018

Cox, Josie, The sharing economy is failing for one simple reason – people can't be trusted, The Independent, July 30, 2017

Dillet, Romain What happened to the sharing economy? Tech Crunch, July 31, 2019

Dimicock, Michael, Defining generations: Where Millennials end and Gen Z begins, Pew Research Center, January 17, 2019

Elmore, Tim, Generation Z Unfiltered: Facing Nine Hidden Challenges of the Most Anxious Population Poet Gardener Publishing, 2020

Fain, Paul, Google Curriculum, College Credit, Inside Higher Ed, September 26, 2018

Feuer, William, Airbnb reportedly lost money last year as costs ballooned ahead of its planned public listing this year, CNBC, February 11, 2020

Florida, Richard, the changing demographics of America's suburbs, CityLab, November 7, 2019

Franchises, Tracy, Hoefel, Fernanda, True Gen: Generation Z and its implications for companies, McKinsey and Company, 2020

Garone, Elizabeth, Women Flock to Franchising, Wall Street Journal, December 1, 2019

Generation Z is stressed, depressed and exam obsessed, The Economist, February 27, 2019

Goldstein, Steve, why Uber and Lyft will fail miserably at autonomous driving, MarketWatch, August 30, 2019

Gorysberg, Boris, Lee, Jeremiah, Price, Jesse and Chengy, J.Yo-Jud, The Leaders Guide to Corporate Culture, Harvard Business Review, January/February 2018

Hall, John, Why you should start considering universities for long term partnerships, Inc., March 17, 2019

Isaac, Mike, Super Pumped the Battle for Uber, Lake Book 2019

Jenkins, Ryan, This is the most in demand skill of the future, Inc. July 22, 2019

Keil, Roger, Suburban change is transforming city life around the world, The Conversation, October 30, 2019

Kiersz, Andy, These are the industries most likely to be taken over by robots, World Economic Forum, April 25, 2019.

Kinder, Molly, Putting the worker in the future of work, Brookings, November 19, 2019

Kolczak, Amy, Five trends influencing the future of our cities, National Geographic, December 8, 2017

Leighton, Heather, How suburbs are turning into hipsturbias to cater to millennials, Ric Kinder Institute for Urban Research, October 1, 2019

Lutchen, Kenneth, Why companies and universities should form long term collaborations, Harvard Business Review, January 24, 2018

Marr, Bernard, The 10 vital skills you will need for the future of work, Forbes, April 29, 2019

Marr, Bernard, The Future of work: 5 Important Ways Jobs Will Change in the 4th industrial revolution. Forbes, July 15, 2019

McBride, Stephen, Uber's nightmare has just begun, Forbes, September 4, 2019

Muniz, Hanna, 17 best college majors for finding a job, Prep Scholar, October 22, 2019

Palmer, Annie, Bosa, Deidre, Airbnb's quarterly loss reportedly doubled in Q1, a bad sign as investors grow wary of money losers, CNBC, October 17, 2019

Paquette, Aaron, Gen Z Is poised to become the most entrepreneurial generation ever - even more so than millennials, VisionCritical, April 28, 2019

Passy, Jacob Gen Z is financial better armed and better educated than millennials were at the same age, MarketWatch, January 29, 2020

Patel, Deep, 8 Ways Generation Z will differ from millennials in the workplace, Forbes, September 21, 2017

Penn, Joanna, Wighbey, John, Uber Airbnb and consequences of the sharing economy, Harvard Kennedy School, Journalists' Resource, June 3, 2016

Preparing for the Future of Work, World Economic Forum, 2020

Rapacon, Stacy, 25 best college majors for a lucrative career, Kiplinger, February 5, 2019

Santana, Gisette, Millennials are flocking to the Suburbs, Rick Kinder Institute for Urban Research, June 5, 2017

Schieber, Jonathan, Uber's losses top $1 billion, better than expected revenues, Tech Crunch November 4, 2019

Smith, Yves, Uber is headed for a crash, New York Magazine, December 4, 2018

Spitznagel, Eric, Generation Z is bigger than millennials – and they're out to change the world, New York Post, January 25, 2020

Staff reporter, Angie's List report first profitable year in company history, IBJ, February 23, 2016

St Esprit, Meg, The stigma of choosing trade school over college, The Atlantic, March 6, 2019

Thiefels, Jessica, 5 simple ways to assess company culture, Achievers, April 24, 2018

Tomar, Dave, Trade schools on the rise: is trade school right for you? The Quad, January 9, 2020

Walker, Alissa, A manifesto for a new suburbia, Curbed, November 11, 2019

Wyckoff, Whitney Blair, The 25 best jobs of 2020, US News and World Report, January 7, 2020

Zimmerman, Eli, Major companies partner with colleges for education opportunities in emerging tech, Ed Tech, July 10, 2018

Index

A

J. C. Wolfe and N. E. Cronin, *Owning Intelligence*,
https://doi.org/10.1007/979-8-8688-2388-6

D

E

F

G

H

I, J, K

P

Q

R

S

T

U, V

W, X, Y, Z

www.ingramcontent.com/pod-product-compliance
Lightning Source LLC
LaVergne TN
LVHW052318200926
848481LV00002B/593
* 9 7 9 8 8 6 8 8 2 3 8 7 9 *